THEMES IN FRENCH CULTURE
A Preface to a Study of French Community

by Rhoda Métraux and Margaret Mead

with an introduction to this edition by
Kathryn M. Anderson-Levitt

Berghahn Books
New York • Oxford

Published in 2001 by

Berghahn Books

www.berghahnbooks.com

© 2001 The Institute for Intercultural Studies

Originally published in 1954 by

STANFORD UNIVERSITY PRESS
STANFORD, CALIFORNIA

© 1954 by the Board of Trustees of the
Leland Stanford Junior University
Library of Congress Catalog Card Number: 53: 11876

Library of Congress Cataloging-in-Publication Data

Métraux, Rhoda Bubendey, 1914-
  Themes in French culture : a preface to a study of French Community / by Rhoda
Métraux and Margaret Mead.
    p. cm. -- (Margaret Mead--researching Western contemporary cultures ; v. 4) (Hoover
Institute studies. Series D, Communities ; no. 1)
  Includes bibliographical references.
  ISBN 1-57181-813-8 (cl. : alk. paper) -- ISBN 1-57181-814-6 (pb. : alk. paper)
    1. France--Civilization. I. Mead, Margaret, 1901-1978. II. Title. III. Series. IV. Series:
Hoover Institute studies. Series D, Communities ; no. 1

  DC33 .M46 2001
  944-dc21
                                                              2001025588

British Library Cataloguing in Publication Data

A catalogue record for this book is available
from the British Library.

Printed in the United States on acid-free paper.

TABLE OF CONTENTS

PART ONE
THEMES IN FRENCH CULTURE, by Rhoda Métraux

PART TWO
THREE BACKGROUND PAPERS

SERIES PREFACE

To celebrate the one-hundredth anniversary of the birth of Margaret Mead, Berghahn Books and the Institute for Intercultural Studies are proud to reissue in 2000-2001 a series of classic works. Written or inspired by Dr. Mead, the materials in these seven volumes investigate the study of contemporary Western cultures.

Most of the world today knows Margaret Mead through her earliest publications, *Coming of Age in Samoa, Growing Up in New Guinea, Sex and Temperament,* and numerous others that examine the peoples of the South Pacific, New Guinea, and Indonesia. Two decades after these pioneering works appeared, Dr. Mead had significantly turned to the study of the contemporary societies of Europe and the United States. Through this later work she gained her widest public audience and arguably became the best known cultural anthropologist who has ever lived. All of these works on contemporary culture, a number of which were originally issued in limited editions, have long been out of print.

The volumes in this series are being issued under the general title Margaret Mead: The Study of Contemporary Western Cultures. It is thought that this will provide a clear identification for the series. However, a more accurate title for the series might be Margaret Mead and Friends. Mead was a great collaborator; in the seven volumes that compose the series, dozens of her contemporaries are represented. One volume, *Themes in French Culture: Preface to a Study of French Community* for example, has as its primary author Mead's close collaborator, the eminent anthropologist Rhoda Métraux, with Mead as second author. Another volume combines Mead's study *Soviet Attitudes toward Authority* with Geoffrey Gorer and John Rickman's *The People of Great Russia,* upon which Mead's study heavily draws.

Mead as solo author is represented in her pioneering critique of American life, *And Keep Your Powder Dry.* The last three volumes in the series, likewise compilations of Mead's solo writings, examine the methodology of studying contemporary cultures, the study of the future, and visual culture-all of which have lasting relevance for today's researchers.

The first volume, *The Study of Culture at a Distance,* is in many ways a key to the entire series. This book, edited by Mead and Métraux, is a "manual" showing the research methodologies of the group of scholars that surrounded them in New York during the 1940s and 1950s. It could be argued that Mead – along with Métraux, Ruth Benedict, Gregory Bateson, and Geoffrey Gorer, among others – was instrumental in founding a true school of anthropological research at that time. More than 120 scholars were associated with this group during its five-year formal existence from 1947-52 as the Columbia University Research in Contemporary Cultures (RCC) project. The number is even larger when one considers that the impetus for the research began in a more informal manner in 1940. Organized by Ruth Benedict, efforts were made to contribute to cultural understanding in order to meet the crisis of World War II. The Institute for Intercultural Studies was founded in 1944 to serve as a home for this research. Aside from Mead, Bateson, Benedict, Métraux, and Gorer, those whose names will be most familiar to anthropologists today are Conrad Arensberg, Alex Bavelas, Jane Belo, Ruth Bunzel, Erik Erikson, Paul Garvin, Ruth Landes, Eleanor Leacock, Vera Schwarz, Y. C. Wang, Eric Wolf, Martha Wolfenstein, and Mark Zborowski. Volumes two through seven of this series all derive in one way or another from the work of this research group. Had the McCarthy era not intervened in the 1950s to spread suspicion and doubt about the virtues of trying to understand foreign cultures on their own terms, this group might still be active today.

One of the most exciting aspects of bringing these works to life again has been to realize the remarkably modem quality of the methodologies developed by Mead and her associates during and immediately following World War II. This group was the first to adopt many of the now commonplace analytic tools of scholars who today identify themselves with cultural studies and media studies. The analysis of film, literature, and public imagery in particular was thoroughly and exhaustively explored in this early research. Although the theoretical goals of Mead and her contemporaries often differed from those of many current students of culture, their methodologies and clear analytic vision could be emulated with much profit by today's researchers.

In fact, their contributions have inspired three generations of intellectuals, though often those who have been influenced by their work are unaware of the source of that influence. Whereas Mead and her colleagues are recognized as public celebrities of the past, among anthropologists today there is a vaguely patronizing attitude toward their work. In short, their intellectual achievements do not receive the attention they richly deserve. Why this is so is a poignant question. It is hoped that the reissue of these important works will help to remedy this oversight.

Acknowledgments and Dedication

I am pleased to acknowledge the help of the following people in making this series possible: Matilde Andrade, Mary Catherine Bateson,

Shannon Carson, Wilton Dillon, Frank Farris, Shirley Gordon, Richard Gould, Katherine Grimaldi, Karen Iny, Philip Leis, Anne Brownell Sloane, and Mary Wolfskill and the staff of the Library of Congress Documents Division where the Margaret Mead Archives are currently housed. I would like to dedicate this series to my mother, Florence Lucille O'Kieffe Beeman, who, as a highly successful professional sociologist and social worker, led me to the works of Margaret Mead and her contemporaries, and ultimately to my own profession as an anthropologist.

William O. Beeman

INTRODUCTION
TO THEMES IN FRENCH CULTURE

Kathryn M. Anderson-Levitt

An Incomplete, Fascinating Experiment

You have never read a book quite like this one.[1] This slim volume represents an unusual experiment in research methods. The experiment used in-depth interviews, projective testing, and the analysis of movies and documents to explore just how accurately researchers could describe a society's culture without actually visiting the society. The experiment happened to take France as its subject, making this a pioneering study of French culture as well.

Themes in French Culture was authored primarily by Margaret Mead's close collaborator Rhoda Métraux. (Métraux was not French but acquired her surname from her French anthropologist husband, Alfred Métraux). The study was originally published in 1954 by Stanford University as one of several Hoover Institute Studies. But Métraux and her colleagues compiled the volume as part of a much more ambitious project, as Margaret Mead explains here in the Introduction. About 120 researchers collaborated from 1947 to 1952 to describe seven cultures in the huge Research in Contemporary Cultures project, which Ruth Benedict launched and Mead organized after Benedict's death in 1948. Benedict and Mead conceived of the project as a response to the experience of World War II and the subsequent Cold War when travel to large parts of the world became impossible.

Mead and Métraux describe the larger study and illustrate its methods in their "manual," *The Study of Culture at a Distance* (1953, republished 2000). There they explain that within the larger project a team of researchers, originally convened by anthropologist Geoffrey Gorer and later by Rhoda Métraux, worked together to study French culture.[2] Reading *The Study of Culture at a Distance* alongside this volume will enrich your understanding of the research and its data, especially because the manual contains two verbatim interviews from the French study and a transcript of a working session during which the team formulated a hypothesis about French culture.

Mead, Métraux, and their colleagues designed this study of France as a case to test their methods, as Mead explains in the Introduction to this volume. France was perfectly accessible, but they deliberately limited themselves to what they could learn by interviewing French individuals in New York City and by studying available movies and documents. They intended to determine "the limitations and possibilities" of study-at-a-distance by comparing the themes identified here with first-hand fieldwork conducted at the same time in France. "Such field work has now actually been done, but is not as yet published, as part of the UNESCO Tensions Project," Mead wrote (Introduction, note 2). Unfortunately, as far as I can determine, the research team never completed the experiment. The companion fieldwork never was published, outside of one preliminary piece by Martha Wolfenstein (1954).[3] UNESCO published over a dozen books in its Tensions and Technology series, including one edited by Mead (Mead, ed. 1953) but none on France.

However, nothing stops us from completing the test ourselves. We can assess the validity of *Themes in French Culture* by comparing it to first-hand studies of France of our own choosing. There are two questions to consider in turn. First, how accurately does this book portray French culture? What does it tell us, then, about anthropological research methods? I will propose some answers to both questions based on my reading of the literature on France, my own ethnographic experiences there, a healthy respect for Mead's research skills, and a fascinated but skeptical view of the culture-and-personality school out of which this project grew. However, the experiment remains open. Other readers can compare this volume with other ethnographies and may draw other conclusions about the usefulness of its research methods.

Premises and Methods

The research methods used here as well as the study's focus on the family made sense within mainstream American anthropology of the 1950s. Métraux and Mead took for granted the loosely psychoanalytic premises of the culture-and-personality school (see Bock 1999). They assumed that family dynamics were a central mechanism in the socialization of individuals into their culture. They also assumed that works of art, legal and moral codes, responses to inkblots, and other forms of individual and group expression revealed cultural meanings that might lie beyond informants' conscious awareness. Thus the themes of French culture described here revolve mainly around family relationships and the ambivalent feelings that these dynamics evoke. The volume does not describe the French economic system, material culture, forms of social organization beyond the nuclear family, or any larger French institutions except, indirectly, schooling.

The Interviews

The core of the book, Chapters 1-3, relies primarily on in-depth interviews with key informants who happened to live in New York City.

Members of the research team conducted interviews in French and English, often repeated interviews, with two or three dozen informants. Neither in this volume nor in *The Study of Culture at a Distance* do Métraux and Mead give us a clear description of the informants. They do not tell us how many people they interviewed—indeed, Mead argues elsewhere that it's not "how many" informants but "what kind" that matters (Mead & Métraux 1953:44).[4] Unfortunately, the authors don't provide a systematic description of "what kind" either. We must piece together from descriptions scattered through *Themes* and *The Study of Culture at a Distance* that informants ranged in age from an "older" couple to a "girl" and included "a father with 18- and 20-year-old sons," "a mother of a 6-year-old son" and a "young bride" (*Themes* p. 52, p. 10, and p. 17). They included a self-made intellectual in his forties, born in the country of petit bourgeois parents, who had not lived in France since 1918, and his wife, born in Paris but from the same social milieu (*Study* p. 182). There was a female *lycée* professor and at least one other teacher (*Themes* pp. 38-39). There was a 30-year-old woman who had left France at the age of 23 (*Themes* p. 18), and the son of an American father raised in France by his French mother, who had served in the U.S. army, was married to a French woman, and was studying at an American university (*Study* p. 188).

In the last of the three Background Papers, Theodora Abel, Jane Belo and Martha Wolfenstein provide a more systematic description of the ten French people to whom they administered projective tests (Ch. 6, note 3), at least six of whom were among the informants interviewed.[5] Their subjects were six women and four men, most born and educated in or near Paris, including seven Catholics, two Jews, and one Protestant and ranging in socioeconomic level "from small bourgeoisie to aristocracy."

The other interviewees, too, came mostly from the bourgeoisie (that is, from the better-educated, more or less urban class), to judge from the hints dropped in *Themes* and *The Study of Culture at a Distance*. Several informants in *Themes* mentioned attending *lycée* (academic high school) and taking the *baccalauréat* exam (the *bachot* or *bac*), the gateway to the bourgeoisie. One man even remarked that his father graduated from the École Normale Supérieure, at least as prestigious as Princeton or Harvard (*Themes* p. 4). Thus the informants represented the most elite 20 percent of the French population.[6] Although Mead says in the Introduction, "our informants came from a great variety of backgrounds … including peasant backgrounds" (note 2), she also admits that all had become urban people. Only one informant is actually described as coming from a non-middle-class background—the woman who learned dressmaking in her youth and who later became a railroad employee (*Themes* p. 46). As for "peasants" (*paysans* in French), interpret the word cautiously because I have heard the label applied to affluent farm owners as well as poor tenant farmers.

The Background Papers

Métraux's chapters also draw on other kinds of analysis, including studies of magazine columns, novels, proverbs, letters to the editor, and other texts.[7] Chapter 2 includes an analysis of several child-care manuals[8] (for a delightful comparison, see DeLoache & Gottlieb 2000). But the principal document study is an analysis by Nelly Schargo Hoyt and Métraux of the debates that took place in 1801-02 on the French Civil Code on adoption. It is fascinating. Rather like the New York interviews, it cites bourgeois speakers and a couple of aristocrats (p. 77). But it offers the most unusual cross-cultural comparison I've ever seen, one built into the data and exploited by the analysts: Napoleon Bonaparte, child of Italian Corsican nobility, represents a contrasting point of view.

The second Background Paper is Martha Wolfenstein and Nathan Leites' analysis of 40 French films, over 30 of which they cite by name. In a contemporary review, David Landes found the film analysis the weakest part of the book (1955:908). I, too, question the Freudian over-interpretation in this section that leads, for instance, to conclusions about the mother-daughter relationship that does not refer to a single film image of an actual mother. Yet the concluding paragraph of this chapter merits close attention. First, it contains a capsule comparison with U.S. and British plots that makes the Frenchness of French plots clear. Then it succinctly lays out a French view of life that meshes with my own impressions: People tend to be realistic; deprivations and rewards may be equally undeserved; there is no supernatural justice, nor is the world arranged to satisfy human wishes, yet life can permit a fragile, brief pleasure.

The final chapter presents findings by Abel, Belo and Wolfenstein from the administration of Rorschach and other projective tests. In *The Study of Culture at a Distance*, Mead remarks that where long interviews are possible, they preclude the need for projective tests (Mead & Métraux 1953:317-19). Nonetheless, this brief chapter makes interesting reading, and Métraux use some of its evidence (for instance, on "immobility") in her core chapters.

The Themes

Métraux and Mead provided no conclusion, but it is simple enough to summarize themes of French culture they identified. They see life as organized around the *foyer*, defined implicitly here as the nuclear family at home. The foyer/family is self-contained, closed to the outside world and autonomous. The small family that makes it up is composed of distinct dyadic pairs. Husband and wife complement each other, he taking care of the family's position in the outside world and she managing almost every decision within the home. In his relationship to the children, the father is distanced and split into a benevolent daytime father and a secret, threatening nighttime figure. The mother both nurtures and disciplines the children. There is a tender rivalry between father and son and an almost explicitly sexual attraction between father and daughter. Mothers admire their sons but experience some rivalry with their daughters. Pairs of brothers and brothers and sisters enjoy a warm, non-competitive relationship but sisters are likely to see each another as rivals.[9]

In their socialization at home and beyond, children learn to hold in their bodies but may exercise verbal aggression and, of course, come to enjoy "the delights of the table" (p. 42). Parents and teachers design education or *formation* to shape the whole person. They seek to awaken the imagination and critical spirit by presenting correct models learned by rote (a paradox from the U.S. perspective). Beyond the foyer, relationships of same-sex friendship and heterosexual love are based on choice, the opposite of the "natural" emotions on which family relationships rely.

How Valid Is This Portrait of French Culture?

We can choose from a multitude of sources to test Métraux and Mead's hypotheses about French culture. For instance, the French have published hundreds of studies of their own national character since the late eighteenth century, dozens in the 1990s alone. However, most are personal essays without much systematically gathered evidence. More relevant are the reactions of French critics to *Themes* when it first appeared and, of course, studies based on fieldwork.

Contemporary French Critics

The French translation of *Themes in French Culture* appeared in 1957 and included 40 pages of critical reactions from a panel of seven intellectuals (Métraux & Mead 1957). Several of the readers praised the study for its objectivity and some remarked on the "banality" of the findings (compare note 4 of the Introduction). *"Tout cela, on le savait"* (We knew all that), complained André Siegfried of the Académie

Française (1957:127), making the kind of critique that tends to reassure anthropologists about the validity of their study.

Most of the French critics felt that the authors were right to focus on the *foyer*. In fact, this is their strongest point of agreement.[10] Wrote Pierre Mantel, President of the Sociological Institute of Le Havre:

> It is remarkable to have put the French "Foyer" at the center of this study and to have made of it an essential theme of our "culture" and of our collective behavior. This is a discovery and a pleasant discovery, for it's not in the familial context that foreigners usually perceive us [in Métraux & Mead 1957:148, my translation].

However, the French critics also questioned the representativeness of the informants and the literary sources in *Themes*. For instance, some considered it rare that a young man would have an affair with an older woman. Some found the monster myths to be very old-fashioned and, in any case, not limited to France. Many pointed out that the study ignores regional, political and religious variation. (Even today, France divides along old political and religious lines, although there is also a new Christian/Muslim divide. During my fieldwork, I met a dedicated Catholic socialist educator and an accountant who denied that anyone could be both Catholic and socialist. I encountered a Communist-run town council providing free after-school care and a bohemian aristocratic family who could name the true successor to the French throne. Before I even went to France I learned not to bring up politics and religion in conversation, and perhaps the Columbia interviewers unwittingly followed the same rule. The critics did not mention ethnic diversity, but that existed too due to immigration from Eastern and Southern Europe during the first half of the twentieth century (Mandrou 1972).

Most importantly, the French critics felt that this volume described only the bourgeoisie. Wrote Gabriel le Bras, a professor from the Faculty of Law in Paris:

> Your brilliant essay captures bourgeois families. Those of the 1920s better than the 1950s. Those in the city better than in the countryside. For ourselves, we would have preferred a series of essays in which you made a distinction between classes, times, and places. We have a hard time recognizing in your family grouping the coalminer, the stevedore, the long-distance shipper. [1957:145, my translation]

In fact, as you see, most of the critics felt this was an outdated portrait of the bourgeoisie. Critic Anne Cavaillat of the Sociological Institute of Le Havre went so far as to identify the description in *Themes* with French bourgeois families of 1850-1914. Long gone were the days when a young woman entered marriage ignorant about sex or when a brother felt he had to protect his sister's virginity. Parents certainly did not arrange marriages in the 1950s and, said the French readers, modern education gave more emphasis to liberty and initiative than acknowledged here.

Studies of the Bourgeoisie

Is *Themes in French Culture* really, then, a description of the French bourgeoisie? I will leave it to you to find novels and early studies to compare *Themes* with the pre-World War I bourgeoisie. Since Métraux and Mead thought they were identifying long-term patterns, let me compare here with more recent and more systematic descriptions. Pierre Bourdieu's *Distinctions* (1984) confirms Le Bras' perception: there really are strong differences in the way the bourgeoisie and the popular classes conduct themselves in France. Bourdieu drew on a combination of survey data and personal observation from the 1970s, but Beatrix LeWita's ethnographic observations of Parisian bourgeois in the 1980s tend to confirm his portrait (LeWita 1994). Both see in bourgeois behavior a deliberate self-control, a reining in of the appetite, in the context of the economic freedom to engage in almost any luxury. Where a working man wolfs down solid portions of beef or pork, the bourgeois man takes minced bites of fish; where a working man blows his nose loudly into a big cotton handkerchief, the bourgeois applies a fragile Kleenex and sniffs (Bourdieu 1984:190-91). Here we see Métraux and Mead's theme of physical control and near immobility applied not to the French in general but to the French bourgeoisie.

Bourdieu and LeWita also point to the bourgeoisie's insistence that form, not just the substance, matters, elaborating on the observations in *Themes* about learning correct models (p. 39). In the all-important realm of food, says Bourdieu, the bourgeoisie will insist that everyone eat the same course of the meal together, whereas in working families the women may move on to dessert while the men eat second helpings of the main course. (I learned the importance of form over substance when I arrived for dinner at a bourgeois home to find that Madame had forgotten the invitation in the hubbub of her daughter's emergency appendectomy. She had almost no food in the house, but she pulled together the form of a correct meal nonetheless, with hard-boiled eggs on a bed of spinach for starters and a spinach omelet as the main dish.)

Lacking a comparative framework, neither Bourdieu nor LeWita comment much on what is specifically French, as opposed to European on the one hand or strictly Parisian on the other, about the patterns they observed. One recent study does make both comparisons.

Michèle Lamont, sociologist from Québec, conducted in-depth interviews with bourgeois/upper-middle-class men from both Paris and New York and from the provincial cities of Clermont-Ferrand and Indianapolis (1992). Her study does echo certain themes from Métraux and Mead: certainly the French men emphasized the well-rounded intellect over specialized expertise, and they still expressed more tolerance of adultery than their U.S. counterparts. Lamont also confirms, in contradiction to the French critics above, that there was more similarity than difference between big city and province in the same country.

However, Lamont focuses on a very specific problem, the bourgeois moral code. Bourdieu and LeWita focus on the work people must do to construct themselves as bourgeois. None of these authors describe the life of the family as Métraux and Mead do. They take us in different directions, as do most ethnographic studies of other segments of French society.

Ethnographies

In spite of *Themes'* narrow sample of informants, legitimately criticized by the French readers, certain ethnographic studies of rural villages located at a great geographic and social distance from the Parisian bourgeoisie nonetheless confirmed some of Métraux and Mead's themes about family. Two ethnographies in particular, conducted about the same time as this study-at-a-distance, offered the same portrait of the nuclear family closed against the "them" outside it. These are *Nouville* by Lucien Bernot and René Blancard (1953) and *Village in the Vaucluse* by Laurence Wylie (1974).

Nouville, the "pioneer" in French village monographs (Cuisinier & Segalen 1986: 40), describes a village in northern France studied in 1949-50. The American culture-and-personality tradition heavily influenced the book, perhaps because ethnologist Bernot teamed up with psychologist Blancard (Bromberger 1987:77). Still, the emphasis is highly unusual in a country where earlier monographs on French villages emphasized folklore and material culture while later studies emphasized social and economic organization (Cuisinier & Segalen 1986). In any case, Bernot and Blancard argued that among workers, farmers, civil servants, managers and independent business people in the village, child rearing stressed external dangers and led to adults who were negative, apathetic, and defensive of *nous* ("us," that is, their family) as opposed to *ils*, "them" at all levels. According to these authors, Rorschach tests revealed a psychological profile "no doubt pathological" in its highly negative Nouville version but recognizable in all Frenchmen (1953 :400).

In *Village in the Vaucluse*, Laurence Wylie described a village of southern France that he studied in 1950-51 and revisited through the following decade. Wylie was an American professor of French civilization rather than an ethnographer. However, when designing his study he consulted with Margaret Mead, Geoffrey Gorer, and other anthropologists in the culture-and-personality school as well as with Lucien Bernot. Like Bernot and Blancard, Wylie identified the theme of the nuclear family opposed to outsiders. His work also echoes Métraux and Mead's discussion of control of physical violence in favor of oral aggression and he, too, describes how young people learned to enjoy food and drink in moderation.

More recent ethnographic research by French and American ethnographers confirms certain themes, such as the appreciation of the pleasures of the table. The theme of "our family versus the world" also tends to recur. Deborah Reed-Danahay (1996) examines farm families of Central France as *les nôtres* (us and ours) opposed to an outside world represented in her book by France's central school system and teachers sent from the city. However, like *Nouville* and *Village in the Vaucluse* before them, Reed-Danahay's study focuses on relations to outsiders, not on dynamics inside the family. These ethnographies are more discrete, as it were, than *Themes in French Culture*. The one rural study that does discuss family dynamics more explicitly, Susan Carol Rogers' study of a village in the Massif Central in the 1970s and 1980s, describes a different family than Métraux and Mead found (1991). In Sainte-Foy, the focus was on the tension between young wife and mother-in-law as the woman marrying in seeks to establish herself a mother—a pattern familiar elsewhere in the Mediterranean and as far away as China, but not like the tight nuclear family described in *Themes*.

Curiously, in my own fieldwork mostly among schoolteachers and other bourgeois families, I did not find families closed in on themselves, although I grant that my research did not examine families systematically. True, high walls and a heavy door protected the house and garden of old bourgeois homes in the central city—but only a low wall revealing the garden ringed homes in the other neighborhoods. Less affluent people lived cramped lives with little privacy in low-rent apartment blocs. The three families I lived with welcomed strangers warmly, although perhaps ethnographers find the exceptional homes. In one high-walled home, Madame invited the boarders to chat and watch television in her master bedroom while she sat on the bed helping her children with homework. In another, Madame had wanted to rent the spare room to a German but settled for the American ethnographer. Nor did I witness middle-class children kept at home; the boys, at least, roamed much more freely than my own children in the pleasant suburbs of their provincial city.

France has also moved toward openness in the three decades I have been observing. There seems to be a more positive attitude toward learning foreign languages and children speak English with much more ease than their parents. There is also a new awareness of France as a multicultural society (van Zanten 1997). Overt racism against North Africans is met with an anti-racist movement as in the organization *S.O.S.-racisme*.

What's Missing

Wylie's fieldwork led to at least one key insight that Métraux and Mead were not in a position to discover. *Village in the Vaucluse* demonstrates the how young people got doubly socialized into "the ideal code which their family and the school have forced on them, and the real code which governs the actions of adults" (1974:120). Young people learned, for instance, that one should respect elderly people, but that everyone makes fun of old Monsieur Maucorps. Citizen should pay taxes, but only those they absolutely cannot avoid. Young people should not have sex before marriage, but girls nonetheless got pregnant and unwed mothers often found good husbands.

My fieldwork inside schools revealed some of the same themes found by Métraux and Mead, but also ones that their interviews had missed. My observations confirmed that French teachers and parents still felt that learning depended on children's effort and that school was supposed to be work, not fun (compare Pitts 1968:295). Teachers still expected school children to sit quietly at their desks longer than American teachers would have, although they also let them run "wild" on the playground. The correct model still mattered to some extent: teachers still demanded neat handwriting and lycée students still learned how to structure a long essay, although teachers also hoped to make school relevant to the child's experience (Anderson-Levitt in press). Thus far, my observations did not range too far beyond *Themes*. But I also learned, as Wylie had observed 25 years before me, that honesty about a child's abilities mattered more than protecting a child's public image. I learned that teachers valued—or had come to value since 1950—a certain degree of "autonomy" or "liberty" for children in the classroom. Most importantly, I learned that teachers and parents highly valued equality, defined as equal treatment, to the point that they questioned the fairness of American reading groups (Anderson-Levitt in press; see also van Zanten 1997). If I had to identify the central themes of French culture, I would certainly include liberty and this particular definition of equality among them.

Many Ways into French Culture(s)

So, contemporary French critics accepted Métraux and Mead's central theme of the *foyer* and its functioning, but only for the bourgeoisie. At the same time, village ethnographies confirmed the theme among peasant families but my own fieldwork leads me to question whether it still applies to the bourgeoisie. Meanwhile, ethnographic studies identified other themes arguably just as central to life in France.

I find I agree with a dissenting interpretation from one of the original French critics, Jean Stoetzel, Director of the French Institute of Public Opinion. Contradicting his colleagues, Stoetzel argued that the *foyer* is not necessarily the central theme in French culture. Although young people rated family values highly on a survey by his Institute, they rated career issues even higher (Métraux & Mead 1957:165). Family is important in France, he argued, but not as important as in a country like Japan. Argued Stoetzel,

> Isn't it possible that other themes, some of them equally central, will be interpreted in France in a manner no less typically French: for example, career, property, politics, not to mention religion? ... It seems to us not at all certain that there is only one way into the spirit of a culture [in Métraux & Mead 1957:167, my translation] .

The wide array of ethnographies of France now available, both in English and French, confirm that there are many ways into French culture. But then, Mead anticipated this argument in the Introduction, where she warned us that here you find "themes, not necessarily *the* themes" of French culture (p. vii).

However, I would take the argument one step further. It's not just that there are many ways into French culture. Rather, it's misleading to think of French culture as a single entity around which we can draw clear boundaries. I would amend Mead's caveat to say that this book describes "themes, not necessarily *the* themes," of "*a*, not necessarily *the* French culture." For my own research on French schoolteachers, I have found it useful to think of culture as knowledge, values and know-how shared by diverse networks of people (Anderson-Levitt in press). Some ideas, such as the definition of equality as equal treatment, may be shared with many residents of France and thus fall more or less within national boundaries. Some, like certain know-how and values for family interaction, may be shared with many other Europeans (or perhaps with the European bourgeoisie but not with the popular classes of France?), as the French critics pointed out (Métraux & Mead 1957). Still other knowledge or values may be shared only with fellow teachers—in France *and perhaps beyond its boundaries*—just as other knowledge and values may be shared with fellow dockworkers in France and elsewhere, or with fellow Catholics, or with fellow farmers. In this sense, there is only one network of cultural knowledge covering the globe, and the ways in which we draw boundaries around parts that we call "national culture" are somewhat arbitrary (Hannerz 1992, Wax 1993).

What Does This Book Tell Us About Research Methods?

The methods used here—in-depth repeated interviews, analysis of historical documents and media studies—did identify certain themes that reverberated with many of the French critics and that found echoes in ethnographic and other studies. By my reading, the experiment did not fail.

In fact, the methods elicited one kind of information very little covered in the ethnographic and sociological studies: discussion of family dynamics and ambivalent feelings about family members. The methods used here seemed to uncover certain aspects of a French experience that ordinary ethnography could not, or that fieldworkers hesitated to share if they did uncover it. In-depth, probing, free-ranging interviews and even responses to wild stimuli like inkblots seemed to elicit a private side to culture that one doesn't often witness during ordinary participant observation. Here, then, are tools for the ethnographic toolkit. Some, such as the study of historical texts and of popular culture have been recently revived. Some, like the "evocative materials" (Mead 1978) we have abandoned along the way, might still prove useful if we apply them creatively and without excessive reverence for psychoanalytic orthodoxy.

On the other hand, the methods for study of culture at a distance cannot be trusted to uncover the whole story. Wylie observed deviations from the cultural ideal that would probably never have been uncovered in interviews. Other ethnographies reveal the messy, concrete textures of life, the many "ways in," that interviews, written texts and films cannot completely capture. This experiment sounds an important warning about relying too exclusively on in-depth interviews or film analysis. Ethnography still teaches us what other research cannot—a point Margaret Mead made in the Introduction and would no doubt have underlined if she and her colleagues had completed this experiment themselves.

Conclusion

I recommend this book to the ethnographer planning research in France, particularly one intending to work with the urban middle class, because it focuses on an intimate side of culture little discussed in other ethnographic studies. It will provoke you to ask questions you might otherwise not have raised. I also hope that students of family dynamics will include this work in building a cross-cultural base for their theories. Finally and most importantly, I hope that a new generation of researchers note the "limits" as well as the "possibilities" of media analysis and in-depth interviews that this book reveals when it is compared, as its authors intended, to findings from fieldwork.

University of Michigan-Dearborn

References

Anderson-Levitt, Kathryn M. 1989. Degrees of distance between teachers and parents in urban France. *Anthropology and Education Quarterly* 20(2): 97-117.

Anderson-Levitt, Kathryn M. in press. *Teaching cultures: Knowledge for teaching first grade in France and the United States.* Cresskill, NJ: Hampton Press.

Beaujeu-Garnier, Jacqueline. 1976. *La population française.* Paris : Armand Colin.

Bernot, Lucien, and René Blancard. 1953. *Nouville : un village français.* Paris : Institut d'ethnologie.

Bock, Philip K. 1999. *Rethinking psychological anthropology*, 2nd ed. Waveland.

Bourdieu, Pierre. 1984. *Distinction : A social critique of the judgement of taste.* Richard Nice, trans. Cambridge, MA: Harvard University Press.

Bromberger, Christian. 1987. Du grand au petit. Variations des échelles et des objets d'analyse dans l'histoire récente de l'ethnologie de la France. *In* Isac Chivas & Utz Juggle, eds. *Ethnologies en miroir* (pp. 67-94). Paris : Éditions de la Maison des Sciences de l'Homme.

Cuisinier, Jean, and Martine Segalen. 1986. *Ethnologie de la France.* (*Que sais-je ?* no. 2307). Paris : Presses Universitaires de la France.

Delmarle, Jean. 1973. *Classes et lutte de classes.* Paris : Éditions Ouvrières.

DeLoache, Judy, and Alma Gottlieb. 2000. *A world of babies: Imagined childcare guides for seven societies.* New York: Cambridge University Press.

Dillon, Wilton. 1969. *Gifts and nations. The obligation to give, receive and repay*. With a foreword by Talcott Parsons The Hague, Paris, Mouton.

Hannerz, Ulf. 1992. *Cultural complexity*. New York: Columbia University Press.

Lamont, Michèle. 1992. *Money, morals, and manners: The culture of the French and American upper-middle class*. Chicago: University of Chicago.

Landes, David. 1955. Review of *Themes in French Culture*. American Anthropologist 57:907-909.

LeWita, Béatrix. 1994. *French bourgeois culture*. J. A. Underwood, trans. Cambridge: Cambridge University Press. [Published in France in 1988 as *Ni vue ni connue: Approche ethnographique de la culture bourgeoise*. Paris : Éditions de la Maison des Sciences de l'Homme.]

Mandrou, Robert. 1972. Les étrangers en France. In Michel François, ed. *La France et les Français*, pp. 1546-1564. Paris : Gallimard.

Mead, Margaret. 1935. *Sex and temperament in three primitive societies*. New York: W. Morrow.

Mead, Margaret. 1949. *Male and female*. New York: W. Morrow.

Mead, Margaret. 1978. The evocation of psychologically relevant responses in ethnological fieldwork. In George D. Spindler, ed. *The making of psychological anthropology*, pp. 87-139. Los Angeles: University of California Press.

Mead, Margaret, and Rhoda Métraux, eds. 1953. *The study of culture at a distance*. Chicago: University of Chicago Press. [reprinted 2000 New York: Berghahn Books].

Mead, Margaret, ed. 1953. *Cultural Patterns and Technological Change: A Manual Prepared by the World Federation for Mental Health*. Tensions and Technology Series. Paris: UNESCO. [reprinted 1955, New York: Mentor].

Métraux, Rhoda, and Margaret Mead. 1957. *Thèmes de "culture" de la France: Introduction à une étude de la communauté française*. Yvonne-Delphée Miroglio, trans. Le Havre : L'Institut havrais de sociologie économique et de psychologie des peoples.

Pitts, Jesse. 1968. The family and peer groups. *In* Normal W. Bell and Ezra F. Vogel, eds. *A modern introduction to the family*, pp. 290-310. New York: Free Press.

Reed-Danahay, Deborah. 1996. *Education and identity in rural France*. Cambridge: Cambridge University Press.

Rogers, Susan Carol. 1991. *Shaping modern times in rural France*. Princeton, NJ: Princeton University Press.

van Zanten, A. (1997). Schooling immigrants in France in the 1990s: Success or failure of the Republican model of integration? *Anthropology and Education Quarterly* 28(3), 351-375.

Wax, M. 1993. How culture misdirects multiculturalism. *Anthropology and Education Quarterly* 24(2), 99-115.

Wolfenstein, Martha. 1955. French parents take their children to the park. *In* Margaret Mead & Martha Wolfenstein, eds. *Childhood in contemporary cultures*, pp.99-117. Chicago: University of Chicago Press.

Wylie, Laurence. 1974 [1957]. *Village in the Vaucluse*, 3rd ed. Cambridge, MA: Harvard University Press.

Notes

1. Thanks to William Beeman, Wilton Dillon, Joseph Gaughan, and Deborah Reed-Danahay for conversations that contributed to the ideas in this essay, although the final interpretation is my own.

2. Gorer is not one of this volume's authors, but his unpublished paper "French culture – Preliminary hypotheses" clearly influenced Métraux, who quotes it on pages 8, 44-45, and 47. Métraux cites twelve members the research team on p. 61, note 1, of this volume.

3. Wolfenstein described her observations in Paris in the summer of 1947 as "preliminary work for a group project on French culture, which began in the fall of that year as part of Columbia University Research in Contemporary Cultures" (1954:99). She cites *Themes in French Culture* but does not cite any other ethnographic work from France. Beginning in 1951, Mead's student, Wilton Dillon, conducted a pioneering multi-level study of France based in part on a life history of a factory owner (Dillon 1969), but his fieldwork was not affiliated with the Research in Contemporary Cultures project (Dillon, personal communication).

4. The archives of the Research in Contemporary Cultures project, now kept in the Mead archives at the U. S. Library of Congress, identify at least 87 interviews of up to 34 informants in the Table of Contents for the French study. An exact count of informants is impossible because some interviews were identified by the informant's initial and others, possibly of the same persons, by a code number, but there were at minimum 17 persons interviewed. Most were interviewed once but eight informants were interviewed repeatedly, from two to fourteen times. Thanks to William Beeman for providing the Table of Contents.

5. According to the Table of Contents in the Library of Congress.

6. In 1954, owners of major corporations, professionals and high-level managers accounted for just 3.4% of the population, middle-level managers for 5.8%, and white-collar employees for 10.8%. In contrast, farmers and agricultural laborers made up 26.7% and the "popular classes" (artisans, small business owners, and blue-collar workers) made up 50.6% (calculated from Beaujeu-Garnier 1976:185). Like other French demographers at that time, Beaujeu-Garnier actually lumped together small business owners and artisans with the biggest industrialists, reporting that this combined group made up 12.0% of the population. Based on a more detailed class breakdown by Delmarle (1973:310-11), I estimate that owners of major corporations made up just 4.2% of this group or, in 1954, 0.5% of the population.

7. According to the Table of Contents in the Library of Congress.

8. These manuals are also archived at the Library of Congress with the other RCC materials.

9. The authors did not explain *why* French family dynamics should fit the pattern described. Mead later offered hints in the film *Four Families* (Canadian National Film Board 1960), in which she compared a French peasant family to peasant/farming families of India, Japan and Canada and showed how the presence of grandparents as heads of the household made a difference in wives' roles. The film also illustrates French training for the delights of the table and the strict control of older children.

   Curiously, these descriptions of family gender roles, which fit the naturalized stereotype of masculine solidarity and feminine competition, passed without critique from the author of *Sex and temperament in three primitive societies* (Mead 1935). By this time, soon after the publication of *Male and Female* (1949), she had apparently tempered her strongly constructivist view of gender roles (Mead 1978:120).

10. Jesse Pitts, another insider to this world, agreed that the center circle of bourgeois life is the nuclear family, which is composed of mother, father, siblings, and probably a servant and is called *"la maison"* (the house) or *"chez nous"* (at our house) (Pitts 1968:294).

INTRODUCTION

This monograph presents a concentrated analysis of certain selected patterns of the culture of France, placed within an anthropological frame-work by an interdisciplinary team. In this final publication form, it has been edited to fit into the research design of this series, also an interdisciplinary enterprise, with a related but not identical set of objectives. Both research backgrounds must therefore be taken into account.

The original research was part of Columbia University Research in Contemporary Cultures, which has been fully described elsewhere.[1] This project was devised so that part of the research was done on inaccessible cultures and part on accessible societies. A deliberate choice was made of French culture as a corrective to the studies of inaccessible societies because French culture was completely accessible to the investigations of French social scientists and to social scientists from other Western countries. We held our investigation to a skeletal form which, however, included the kinds of research we were using on other cultures: anthropological interviewing of living informants in the United States, analysis of historical documents, analysis of current films, use of projective tests, exploration of literary sources, etc., without extensive elaboration of any of these. But we were conscious throughout that such a study of the cultures was properly preliminary to actual field work in French communities.[2] This study, then, stands as an example of what can be done at a distance and, on the basis of comparison with detailed field work, should illustrate the limitations and possibilities of one kind of anthropological work as compared with the other.

This is a matter of more than immediate political importance, as we attempt to apply the kind of understanding to which disciplined knowledge is essential, in fields where such knowledge cannot be obtained – to all the countries behind the Iron Curtain. Also, in attempting to obtain a working understanding of many groups of people, whose political institutions and technological status have changed with great rapidity, it will be necessary, or at least most desirable, to be able to reconstruct cultures which are no longer amenable to direct field methods – such as, for example, that of pre-Communist China, or many parts of present-day India, for which no early field work is available. Methods which combine the use of documentary sources and isolated living informants, whose characters were formed within the vanished culture of earlier regimes, or in communities which have ceased to exist as wholes, will be continuingly valuable in all contemporary research in a rapidly changing world.

France seemed ideally suited to such a research project: stable and intact within long-recognized boundaries, with a history profusely and critically documented, with a group of social scientists interested in applying new interdisciplinary methods. It is within this context that we are presenting here – as a type exploration of cultural themes relevant to the understanding of the French community – those patterns of human relationship traditionally fostered within the household and the family, which are basic also to an understanding of the French sense of nationality and civilization and the role of France in the modern world community.

The position of this monograph in this series indicates that we do not claim for this type of analysis either exhaustiveness or exclusiveness. It is a study of themes, not necessarily *the* themes, basic not in the sense that they underlie an entire structure, but only in the sense that from them it is possible to derive many other useful propositions about French culture and to construct working models of future French behavior. Such models make it possible, for example, to discuss the difficulties that are likely to arise if Frenchmen are included in training situations abroad; to throw light on the specific character of the responses of French statesmen to occasional exclusion from Allied councils during and since World War II; or they may serve to clarify the relationship of metropolitan France to those overseas territories for which the French have, at different times and under various circumstances, assumed a national responsibility. Many types of approach are essential to build more complete models. In order to tap even the full possibilities of the anthropological approach alone, we need field work in selected French communities, chosen regionally and with due regard for religious and occupational differences, in which the interaction of identified persons – known in all their living individuality – could be studied in context; so the position of "father" would be studied as embodied in the persons of many contemporary Frenchmen who were fathers – and notaries, schoolmasters, shopkeepers, peasants, artisans, and industrial workers as well. After such a study had been made, carefully controlled statistical samples of the incidence of certain attitudes, as well as an analysis of the patterns of behavior in these different structural positions, would be necessary. The accompanying monographs on France by members of the RADIR Project illustrate the use of other techniques, some of which can quantify certain aspects of the culture.

Our use of historical material in this monograph has been essentially synchronic. We selected one set of historical documents, the reports published in 1805-8 of the discussions by the Conseil d'Etat of the new codification of laws for the *Code Civil,* and analyzed certain sections the content of which paralleled our contemporary materials. These verbatim reports, even more than the reports of the Commission for the reform of the *Code Civil* with which some comparisons were made, are peculiarly suited to anthropological methods of interaction analysts because – as is so often not the case – each speaker is identified in sequence so that part of the original interpersonal interchange is preserved. This paper on the *Code* however, is primarily designed as a demonstration of how anthropological analysis may be applied to historical documents and is used as material on French cultural attitudes which seem, on the basis of limited research, to have existed for quite a long time. But such a study of stability in culture is only part of the contribution which would be expected from an historical analysis of trends in which both stabilities and changes would be identified.

This monograph represents, furthermore, only the first stage of cultural research, the stage in which themes are identified. Each of these themes – or any cluster of these themes, such as, for instance, the conception of the *foyer* as the model for a closed circle of relationships, the tendency for relationships within the *foyer* (and elsewhere) to have an exclusive dyadic form, the compartmentalization of relationships and areas of interest and shared communication, the handling of danger by externalization and distantiation on and the reciprocal fear of destruction by the intrusion of the distantiated, etc. – could be pursued backward in time or contemporaneously in different materials. As the emphasis is upon French culture as relevant to the understanding of national and international behavior, we have not specified class or regional versions of French national culture, although every concrete illustration is inevitably localized in time and space, by class and region, by religion and occupation and political affiliation.[3] If we had derived a theme exclusively from informants from Provençe or from the writings of a special school of novelists of a given period, it would be legitimate to raise the question of whether there was any reason to say that this particular theme was French without inspecting other regions, other schools, or other periods. But the examples which are presented here are illustrations, chosen after the themes had been identified. This applies particularly to illustrations taken from the work of creative artists who may provide the most vivid and concise statement of a theme which has been laboriously derived from many sources.

A second difficulty of presentation comes from the requirement that statements about a contemporary culture must be made in terms which are acceptable to members of that culture. This means that the extent to which they appear to be statements of any importance is a function of the level of articulateness in the culture. In Anglo-Saxon countries, there has been little premium on explicit recognition of the sort of cultural themes with which this type of anthropological research has been concerned. Statements about the reversal of filial and parental roles as between England and America, making the child the exhibitionist to his father's spectatorship in America, the spectator to his father's exhibitionism in England, can come as somewhat illuminating, as a level of abstraction about human relationships which is unexpected and hence fresh and interesting. In a culture as explicitly formulated as that of France, new statements must run a double hazard: if they are phrased in culturally acceptable terms they may sound so familiar as to appear to be truisms, and stale truisms at that; or, if their deviation from the traditional is conspicuous, they may be immediately disputed as untrue or at least un-French, something that might perhaps at best have some immediate comprehensibility to a foreigner looking *at* France.[4]

If, however, in order to highlight the analysis, attention is focused by repetition of a word or phrase which is ordinarily taken for granted – as has been done in this study in the use of the word *foyer* to focus attention upon the organization of the French household – here again there may be an objection that it is un-French to use the word as often and in these contexts. We have been continually faced with the fact that certain French words, like *foyer,* more inclusive and excluding than any English term, and *civilisation,* with greater extension in time and space, cannot be translated into English, and that two words on which this type of analysis relies heavily, *culture* and *pattern,* have no counterparts in French vocabulary or French thought. These problems of nonequivalence in vocabulary and of divergence or delayed convergence in theory are problems for future collaboration between anthropologists of different nationalities, The ultimate solution of how cultural analyses are to be both so familiar as to be greeted as accurate and so unfamiliar as to be greeted as new and therefore worth the effort by which they were achieved, must be different for each culture and will require co-operation from anthropologists within the culture working with anthropologists of other nationalities.

This monograph then is a study of thematic regularities in French culture which have been identified by a group working together on a variety of materials, cross-checking patterns found in one set of materials against patterns found in another – between an informant's account of her parents' attitudes toward quarreling, a foreign observer's comments on French violence, the responses of French subjects to projective tests, the analysis of the plots of recent French films, and so on. The materials developed by the different members of the research team were all processed and shared and are available in the files of Columbia University Research in Contemporary Cultures, now located in the custody of the Institute for Intercultural Studies, where a master set of these papers, with references to each original unpublished document, is to be found.

Part One has been organized so as to give a coherent presentation, drawing on the range of materials, of a series of themes important in the nexus of familial relationships in the home, in the education of the French child for its adult role, and in the formation of attitudes that guide individuals, growing to maturity, as they move out of the *foyer*. Part Two contains background papers, using specific materials, whose authors played a central role in the French research group. From Geoffrey Gorer's original formulations at the close of the first phase of the research work, when he was the convener of the group working on France, a number of verbatim selections have been chosen for incorporation into Rhoda Métraux's paper. Dr. Métraux was the convener of the group during its second phase and has taken the responsibility for the organization of the material with periodic consultation with the other members of the group. My own role has been limited to membership in the group working on France, an original responsibility for the mechanics of the research design of the larger project and, following Professor Benedict's death, responsibility for the direction of the project of which this work on France was a part.

Harold Lasswell has stressed the extent to which, as ties become world-wide, local awareness is intensified. As our political forms and our technology become more uniform, the significance of national cultural styles becomes greater. The differences among the ways in which Frenchmen and Germans, Englishmen, and Italians view human relationships in the family, the community, the nation, and the world, become differences to be taken into account in predicting whether an international conference will fail or succeed or in gauging the chances which any international plan has for acceptance. Since the United States and Asian countries have become factors to be reckoned with in world politics, members of European countries have become more conscious of themselves as European, and it may be expected that within each political ideology the sense of the Frenchness of the French version, the distinctive Italian quality of the Italian version will also be stressed. This increased self-awareness and self-scrutiny in turn becomes a factor in the intensification of the uniqueness of French cultural behavior. Thus, in any attempt to establish a world community, it becomes more, not less, important to become sensitively aware, in ways which can be explicitly formulated and subjected to processes of validation and verification, of the pattern of culture of each society of which that world community is to be composed.

Margaret Mead

New York
February 15, 1952

NOTES

1. Cf. Margaret Mead, "Columbia University Research in Contemporary Cultures," in *Groups, Leadership and Men,* edited by Harold Guetzkow (Pittsburgh: Carnegie Press, 1951), pp. 106-17.
2. Such field work has now actually been done, but is not as yet published, as part of the Unesco Tensions Project.
3. Our informants came from a great variety of backgrounds; in this study, however, it was inevitable that all, including those of peasant backgrounds were urban or urbanized people.
4. This reaction to a paper written from this material was reported by Dr. Claude Lévy-Strauss at the International Conference on Anthropology, held at the Wenner-Gren Foundation in June 1952; the French students were indifferent, the foreigners illuminated.

Part One

THEMES IN FRENCH CULTURE

I. The Foyer: The World Within

The Frenchman at home is *chez-soi,* in his own place. For the French, *le foyer* is *un petit bien complet, un petit bien indépendent* – a small possession, complete and independent. But *bien* means not only possession or, more specifically, a piece of property; it also conveys, among other meanings, those of comfort, excellence, and well-being, all of which – together with the idea of its privacy and autonomy – combine in the feeling about *le foyer.*

The term is an untranslatable one; to render it inadequately as *house* or *home* or *family,* with the connotations these words have for Americans, is to distort the total meaning which *le foyer* has for those who belong to it. It is a truism that this is a little used word in French daily conversation and, from one point of view, a discussion of French family life is itself an anomaly. For, generally speaking, this is a subject which in its intimate details is reserved to those close to the family and, as an entity, to formal, even solemn public occasions. As one Frenchman commented:[2]

> Anyone who insists on talking about *le foyer* on any and every occasion must be either a politician or a pompous fool to whom one reacts with irony.

Explicitly he referred to the use of the term; implicitly – for he went on to speak of *le foyer* as a political symbol – he expressed a protective attitude toward a discussion of the subject itself. At the same time, a clear view of *le foyer* is crucial to an understanding of French national culture and the French self-image whether one is concerned with the individual or with the place of France, as seen by the French, in the contemporary world. Here I shall be concerned not with these broader implications, but rather with the actual *foyer.*[3] The necessary repetitions of the descriptive term – where the French conception is meant – place this study outside, at some distance from the culture described.

The arrangement of French dwellings conveys something of the distance between the world without and the world within the *foyer.* One need only recall houses in provincial France where a high wall, enclosing the garden or the court behind or the plot of land around the house, shuts out too-curious neighbors and passers-by; where a bell on garden gate or door rings, perhaps automatically, to announce each person – stranger or member of the family – who approaches; where every footfall around the house sounds on gravel. Or one may visualize the urban apartment building where the incomer must first pass the sharp scrutiny of the *concierge* next to the entrance before proceeding up briefly lighted stairs, to the door of his destination. Designs of nineteenth-century luxury apartments in Paris provide another, although somewhat different, image of the privacy of the *foyer*. Here each apartment occupies an entire floor of a building which also, on the first two floors, houses a business establishment and, in the attics, has rooms for servants and poor tenants. The close proximity of these unrelated worlds implies the detachment of each from the other. The specific image alters from one type of house, from one region of France to another. Common to them is the sense of the boundary set, the protection against possible intrusion. Not everyone, by any means, owns a house, a garden, or a plot of land; on the contrary, housing is a major problem in France today (including both the provision of housing in crowded cities and the utilization of antiquated housing in provincial towns). But ownership – and the maintenance of privacy and independent security – is something which the adult desires and expects: a home is inherited, bought or worked towards for eventual retirement, ideally, though it may not be attained in fact.

The household, established at marriage, is intended to have permanence. The furniture and appliances that are then installed are meant to last not until a change in fashion but throughout a lifetime. For the home, however agreeable, is arranged neither for extensive display nor as a meeting place with outsiders, but chiefly to please the taste and to suit the convenience of those who live in it. However, the house (or the apartment) is not in itself the *foyer*. In its figurative sense – and this is the way in which it is most commonly used – *le foyer* refers to a group of people – a married couple and their children – who live together in a fixed place and form a closed circle.

The image of the circle, with its implication of closure, is one that is used by the French to describe social groups to which they belong. (*Milieu* refers to the context; *cercle* to the structure of a group.) *Cercle* is, for instance, commonly part of the name of clubs (e. g., in almost any town there is a *Cercle militaire* for veterans, etc.). It is also used in a generally descriptive way. So, in speaking of his father's position, a man says:

> After he finished the École Normale Superieure ... he immediately entered the class or *circle* which in France is called *les Universitaires*. It is a class of people very much apart from the rest of the population and very self-contained.

Or, comparing her French and American experiences, a woman says:

> There are many *circles* in France, but these are all completely closed groups. In America there are clubs whose sole purpose is to permit

strangers to make acquaintanceships. That simply doesn't exist in France. There one participates in a group simply because one belongs to it as, for example, I belong to the university group, to another group of the family, and equally to a Protestant religious group. The people of these different circles do not mix at all (*ne se mélangent pas du tout*). I have two uncles who are polytechnicians, but I see them only in their capacity as uncles in our family circle, never as polytechnicians in the company of other members of their profession …

Thus, the adult through his different associations and interests belongs to various "circles," each of which, in the sense of being self-contained, both closes in its members and keeps strangers out.

Of these circles, the family – especially the *foyer* – is the most self-contained and enduring in that family relationships are regarded as all but indestructible and the individual's obligations to and benefits from the immediate family continue throughout life. For the child (especially the girl) who has grown up and become independent, the door to the parental home remains "always open"; reciprocally, parents feel that they have a continuing right to participate in major decisions made by their grown children that may affect the larger family. Parents and children have a mutual responsibility for each other's well-being that is reflected in legal arrangements about inheritance and the care of the indigent: parents cannot disinherit children nor can children disclaim responsibility for the care of elderly or ailing parents. Yet, ideally, reciprocity consists not in making return gifts for what has been received, but in protecting what one has and passing on to the next generation what one has received and cared for. Thus, the past is continually made part of the present and the *foyer,* like other social circles, is not isolated but is one of an interlocking series.

The larger family (*la famille, les parents*) – including grandparents, parents' siblings, cousins, and so on, as well as those who have married in – is regarded as having unity as it also has extension in time. But in fact, when "the family" is referred to, it is usually the members of the *foyer* and the closest, most congenial relatives and those from whom one expects to inherit (or to whom one expects to bequeath) who are meant. The household itself reflects something of this larger family with its extension over time. Describing what she misses in the American family, a young war-bride writes:[4]

> One doesn't find that good French family tradition; the habits, the reminders (*souvenirs*), the family pictures, the family house and furniture. The family in the United States is in the present. In France, it is in the present, but in the past and future also.

The traditional symbol of the unity of the larger family and its exclusiveness is the *conseil de famille* (family council), which links together the several related *foyers*. Meeting formally or informally, this group may act for its members and in certain situations can be a legally responsible intermediary between the family and the rest of the world. Here the individual may ask advice from or may be called upon to give account to members of his family acting in concert.

Entrance into the family, except by birth, is hedged in with complex legalities intended both to protect the individual who enters and the family whose composition is thereby changed. Doubt and uncertainty about the relationship of the newcomer – the outsider – to the family is expressed most openly in French attitudes towards adoption, which appear to have been extremely consistent during the 150 years since adoption laws were first enacted in the Civil Code. The men who framed the Civil Code in 1801–2, in their discussions of proposed laws of adoption, raised issues that continue to trouble contemporary Frenchmen: can the ties to the family of origin ever be broken? can the tie between adopted child and adoptive parent(s) bind a whole family? which is more effective – the training given a child or its deepest emotions? what would happen if the adopter were later to have children of his own? if the foster child were to be returned to its natural family?[5] So, for instance, in the original discussions of proposed laws, a speaker describes a possible situation in a *foyer*:[6]

> … The (adopting) father often makes way for regrets, the more violent because they are without remedy. A couple have no children. One of them dies. The other remarries. There are children. One can easily imagine the regrets in having given them a stranger for a brother. This is where one will see how far adoption is from imitating nature. Hatred will spring up between the father and the adopted son, between the latter and the natural children; from it will come discord which will trouble the entire family for a long time …

He then goes on to discuss the position of the adopted child in the larger family:

> The adopted child will have rights only on the goods of the adopter ? Then the child becomes a monstrous being in society: he is cut off from his own family and yet he does not belong to his adoptive family. Will he have all the rights of natural children? In that case, the legislator is unjust towards the relatives of the foster father, and more liberal than he has a right to be …

Even today, only those couples who have no prospects of having children of their own can adopt a child;[7] and only recent legal reforms have made it possible for a child to pass completely from its family of origin into its adoptive family.[8] The emphasis in both situations is upon the protection of the *foyer*. Likewise, the rationale of the present government-supported program of adoption for foundlings and abandoned children is the creation of a complete *foyer*. Thus, a pamphlet explaining the new adoption laws states on its cover: "Make a happy adoption. Give a family to the little one who has no relatives. You will install *bonheur* in your *foyer*." Urging adoption upon those who have no children, the pamphlet states:

> … among the numerous children entrusted to the Public Assistance, it is always possible to find beautiful babies, lively (*éveillés* – awakened), lovable and healthy, ready to love those who love them. Adoptions sincerely desired will succeed perfectly, because a beautiful child will quickly bring to a *foyer,* which before its coming was empty *(vide),* a plenitude of joy and *bonheur*.

In the situation presented, each partner to the adoption satisfies an otherwise unfulfillable need of the other: the child has no relatives, there is a void in the adult *foyer* – what is pictured is the creation, not the alteration, of a family. In this situation "adoptions … will succeed perfectly."

The *foyer* that is established at marriage is, ideally, autonomous. The fact that actual independence may be postponed or renounced until the death of the parents (as when a peasant son continues to live with his own family in his parental *foyer)* does not detract from this conception, as it concerns the intimate relationships of husband and wife and children to one another.

From the first, where the *foyer* is concerned, husband and wife are regarded as parents; that is, the *foyer* is visualized as if complete. So, for instance, a French girl and her mother discuss the family:

Daughter (who has grown up abroad, but in a French milieu): … Well, a family is composed of – a man and his wife.

Mother (who grew up in France): No, it is a *mother* and *father.*

Daughter: Well, when it first begins it is a man and wife.

Mother: When you speak about a *family,* you say a mother and father, you never say husband and wife.

Daughter: Suppose they have no children …

Mother: You are speaking about a *family.* It is mother and father …

Parents welcome children warmly and responsibly. With their birth, the human plan of the *foyer* is realized. Yet, though desired and loved, the child is regarded as a heavy charge upon its parents, for its upbringing requires foresight and long years of patient effort. Men and women alike stress the vital importance of bringing up the child properly *(élever l'enfant proprement)*; they point out, besides, that all parents, according to their means, want to do well *(faire quelque chose de bien)* for each child. Consequently, people feel one should be able to decide upon the number of children one wishes to have and – though informants are quick to point out that they themselves know of large families – the general expectation is that the family will remain small. So, one woman says:

> The French woman loves to bring up her children; she has a taste for education. Maybe she wants to concentrate on one or two children and feels she cannot do so well if she has many ...

And a young man comments:

> As for the desire not to have many children, I think the real reason lies in people's mentality. They think it is stupid and without profit for them to have too many children. The general desire is to have two, a girl and a boy. But children are a burden because they must be well brought up; they must be well dressed and taught manners. Nothing is excused. They are taught how to be polite, well mannered *(bien tenu)*. The respect for the child is a real social attitude in France ...

An older man places the same problem in a broader context when he says:

> A Frenchman does not live in the moment. For a Frenchman life is more profound and ample *(plus large)*. He has a view of life *totale et en profondeur* – a more global attitude towards life [than the American]. One doesn't think of one's own life, but of that of one's children, first and foremost ...

The expectation then is that the *foyer* will remain small but that it is complete only when it has its full complement of two generations.

Within the *foyer* pairs of individuals are linked in special relationships, these dyads together forming a nexus of relationships. Ideally, there are eight such dyads: husband and wife, father and son, father and daughter, mother and son, mother and daughter, brother and brother, sister and sister, brother and sister. Discussing these dyadic relationships in an unpublished paper, Geoffrey Gorer comments:[10]

> Valued emotional complexity develops in those situations where the whole group are interconnected through mutual dyadic relationships over a long stretch of time. As the nexus of dyadic relationships becomes

thinner, so does the emotional intensity towards, and the integration of, the individual who has fewer such connections: thus more distant relatives, children's spouses, and so on, are less valued because their enduring relationships are only with some members of the *foyer*.

Each of the familial dyads – as a pair – has its own interests, experiences, and knowledge not shared with the others but respected by them. For example, parents do not share their mutual financial responsibilities with their children; children are expected to accept and respect decisions made by their parents regarding the expenditure of money. However, a daughter may confide some wish to her mother, knowing that the mother will remember it in coming to a decision with the father (though she may well not discuss with him the wish expressed by the daughter). In each relationship there are also recognized areas of reserve between the partners – knowledge and experience not shared within the dyad because private to other relationships into which each partner enters. Thus, trust between husband and wife is not broken when father and son share knowledge or experience not shared by either with the mother. In any one relationship, the partners know what is relevant to both of them; what they do not know – as a pair – is not therefore essentially unknowable but, known to others, is irrelevant to that relationship. Thus, a secret is not unknowable, but knowledge which is selectively shared and protected by the outsider (who does not know) as well as by the participants. The individual, as an individual, decides what he will share and with whom, with the expectation that this choice will be respected by everyone.

In the *foyer* mutuality and trust are built upon an acceptance of both the known and the unknown: upon a willingness to give and receive information on which both partners in a dyad will act in this and other relationships and also upon a willingness to accept actions by each partner based on information not equally available to both. So, while there is a shared common fund of knowledge about everyone in the family, each person also has a combined knowledge of the other members which only he (or she) can integrate and each is known to the others through a series of such combinations. In this way each dyad gives strength, richness, and significance to all the others, reinforces and is reinforced by all the others, and the whole derives its security from the participation of each individual in his (or her) several reciprocal relationships.

Fundamental to the French conception of personal relationships in general is the idea of reciprocity: a personal relationship is, in effect, a dialogue in which *each speaker* responds to the other and provides the necessary clue to the next response. Knowing how to act in a situation with another person includes an expectation of response and the development of a living relationship depends upon the active participation of both persons involved and upon the sensitive awareness each has of the clues provided by the other. For instance, speaking of courtship situations, an informant, a man, comments:

> The incessant play between men and women in France is expressed in a number of patterns such as the man kissing the woman's hand and the woman smiling. The French woman lets a more seriously courting man know by imperceptible signs whether she is willing or not to go further …

Thus, in a love relationship, the woman arouses the love of the man and he, in turn, arouses the love of the woman, in a step by step development in which both take part, reciprocally setting the pace and style. A dramatic counterpoint to this, usually with tragic implications, is the theme – often developed in French films – of the man who falls in love with and is unable to detach himself from a woman who is, however, unresponsive.[11]

The idea of progression through reciprocal action is also integral to French anxieties about quarrels and about fighting: once *both* persons become involved in a quarrel or a fight, there is no telling, people feel, where it may end. Part of the pleasure in *repartie* lies in the mutual recognition and rapid avoidance of danger; there is, however, the phrase *"la parole qui tue"* (the word that kills) which suggests, figuratively, the extreme possibility. (However, to "kill" with words is permissible; to goad a person to physical aggression is not. It should be remembered that French dueling was a highly formalized performance that measured the participants' control as well as skill.) Children are, from a very young age, restrained from aggressive acts that might lead to fighting in retaliation. Discussing the fact that children are not permitted to fight, a mother describes how her six year old son came home from his (American) school covered with bruises:

> She was sure that he had provoked the anger of the other boys and had done something really wrong … It took her some time … to realize that in America she was expected to "encourage my son to fight, to defend himself (à se battre, à se défendre) …"

Significantly, this mother at first assumed that her son had *provoked* an attack by doing "something really wrong."

How dangerous mutual aggression is felt to be, can be inferred from a young man's description of actual fighting when, intending to make one point (i. e., no one in France gets hurt in fights), he implies the opposite (i. e., you could kill):

There's a difference between France and America in another respect too; that is they [in France] can't fight overtly. There is no more the *épée,* no more the pistols ... The upper class now, the bourgeoisie has nothing but a lot of insults: You insult him, he insults you, and you continue and continue but nothing happens ... Of course, there are times when fighting is permissible, like when you get your *bachot* [baccalaureatel; then you are expected to have fights with the police ... It's a free-for-all. But no one is hurt. Never in these times is anyone really hurt like here ... And then when there are strikes in a factory ... no one is ever killed, not like here. I remember the 10th of November 1936, when ten men were killed. It created a terrible drama in France ... Now during the Resistance, then you could kill, that was different, you were expected to ...

Thus, while the reciprocal exchange of insulting words is safe (i. e., "nothing happens"), the quarrel that shifts to "overt fighting" – in fantasy at least – is likely to go to extremes.[12]

These two situations – courtship and quarreling – are only particular instances illustrating the general expectation that each relationship, each situation between two persons, depends for its development upon mutual interaction.[13]

Within the *foyer,* the emotional basis of the several relationships is regarded as "instinctive" and "natural," and the expected emotions are, as it were, paired. A father naturally feels "tenderness" for his child; a child feels "respect" for its father. Both members of a dyad are expected to be guided in their own actions and to interpret each other's behavior in terms of such emotions. The correct expression of the appropriate emotions must be learned by the child – by watching its parents in their relationship to each other, by its own relationship to each of them, and through its early experiences with siblings and cousins while it is still living almost wholly within the safe confines of the immediate and the wider family circle. A necessary part of the child's learning is that explosions can occur that may cause rifts in relationships and that these are a threat, but that the danger can be averted as long as a relationship can be restored and maintained through appropriate behavior. For it is assumed that, in general, members of the family – if they have learned how – will again feel and act upon the tenderness and respect and affection that are inherent in a relationship. The existence of these instinctively felt, positive emotions gives assurance that the relationships of the *foyer* have a permanent security. Not to feel them would be to approach the unnatural or the monstrous; doubt as to their dependability between "relatives" by adoption is a further expression of the concern felt about the outsider who has been drawn into the family circle.

As each individual in the *foyer* plays an essential part in its total integration through his (and her) special relationships to every other person, each is also regarded as unique and irreplaceable. No one can, except in the most limited way, take over the part of someone else. In these circumstances, the absence of any one of the persons making up the *foyer,* or the failure of one of them to fill his (or her) expected role is a potential danger to the whole as it is to each individual who is part of it. For example, two women (in a group interview) comment upon the effect on family life and on the individual member of the family in situations where an elder sister has been obliged to take the place of the mother. One says:

> It is the mother who creates the warmth of the *foyer,* who is responsible for the spirit *(l'esprit)* ... The oldest girl never takes the place of the mother. Sometimes she cooks and cleans, but she can't replace the mother spiritually. She can do all the material things, but nothing more. Look at my sister. When my mother died, she did the work at home, but she couldn't do the other things. Now look, none of us stayed at home ...

That is, the *foyer* collapsed. A little later, the other says:

> When my mother died, B – (eldest sister) ... did not have to take care of us, but she did so at enormous sacrifice. She did something which no ordinary person would do ... [Details omitted.] She gave us all that, but she was never like a mother. She was cold, cold as a stone; everything was done in cold blood. I never knew what a mother was. And I suffered because of it. Perhaps I am today what I am because of that ...

That is, in spite of having been given care, the child did not – in the opinion of the adult remembering her motherless childhood – become the person she might otherwise have been.

On the other hand, one partner in a dyad can help the other fill – or in the eyes of others, appear to fill – his (or her) expected role. So, presenting the father's actions to his children in the best light, the mother not only protects both by preserving the image of what a father should be, but also may help the man to act as a father should. Something like this is implied in a young man's description of his parents' happy relationship, when he says:

> I never heard quarrels *(discussions)*. Even when I heard them at night – I was in the next room – never quarrels. It was due to the very conciliatory character of my mother. My father, on the contrary, was very violent. She dominated it (i. e. his violence).

The attempt by one person (often it is the mother who is so pictured) to preserve the unity of the *foyer* by fostering an illusion about another, and the consequences of disillusionment when the real situation becomes known, is a recurrent theme in French fictional treatment of family life.[14] At such moments of revelation – when the structure of the illusion has broken down before discovered reality – the resolution of the problem may depend upon the willingness (or unwillingness) of all those involved nevertheless to preserve the illusion as a form of reality. In such fictional handling of failure to fulfill expected obligations, the point is not that one person can adequately replace another but, on the contrary, that one person by the exercise of great skill can succeed (or, lacking skill or willingness, can fail) in creating an illusion about the other; then, where the illusion is accepted, all appear to be acting out their proper roles and the integrity of the *foyer* is preserved. In such a situation, the son, for instance, may learn what a father is, not through his own father's behavior, but rather through an interpretation of that behavior given by the mother to protect the dignity of the one and the trust of the other.

In the *foyer* not only is each individual unique, but each relationship – each dyad – has characteristics differentiating it from the others. It is only by experiencing all of them that the growing child becomes able to handle human relationships and, in this sense, also becomes fully human. As a participant in several dyads, the child learns how to interact with differently defined persons, older and younger than himself, how to compartmentalize experience and channel expression of feeling, how to deal with what he is expected – and also with what he is not expected – to know, etc. He learns, furthermore, about the complex relations of performer and observer, actor and audience, that is, about the various roles played by the *third* person to any dyad.

The importance of the *foyer* in developing and protecting the full humanity of the individual is reflected in attitudes towards those who have no *foyer* or whose *foyer* is, for some reason, incomplete. Those who may never have belonged to a *foyer* (the orphan and the illegitimate child) and those who, as adults, do not have a *foyer* to belong to (old maids, bachelors, childless widows, and widowers) are regarded not merely as unfortunate, but also as somehow different in their character from other people. They may never have learned or they may have lost, temporarily perhaps, the faculty of interaction and so, in some manner or degree, seem to be lacking in full humanity.[15]

In fiction, such figures may be treated as comic, as pitiable, or as contemptible, as potential victims of unprovoked hostility or, on the contrary, as persons who will inevitably seek to victimize others – as dangerous strangers.[16] When such persons are represented fictionally, the plot does not necessarily turn upon their isolated situation, but rather upon their character, that is, upon what their situation has made of them as persons.[17] Where an adult is concerned, the relationship of character to the ideal image of the *foyer* may be entirely implicit; where a child is concerned, it is likely to be made rather explicit.[18]

Thus, in the French view, the responsible, rewarded and rewarding adult is a person who has been formed by participation in a *foyer* and who, in turn, provides for the next generation in a *foyer* of his own. Neither the conception of family life as something exclusive and apart nor the emphasis upon the family as the vital factor in the attainment and maintenance of adult status, are peculiarly French. In these conceptions as in many of their attitudes towards the family, including in a general way attitudes towards the relationship of adult and child, the French are also Europeans, sharing in a common cultural tradition. What is peculiarly French is rather the way in which such common elements are recombined, selectively emphasized and interpreted by individuals who are unmistakably members of a culture consciously regarded as unique.

It is in this light, as well as with full awareness that in speaking of personality the French stress the uniqueness of each mature individual, that the organization of the *foyer* should be regarded. In describing this organization in terms of the dyadic relationships of the several pairs of members, both the individual and the family group as a whole are subordinated. Yet each dyad, treated here as a unit, consists of individuals and is part of the whole. Each individual is both actor and audience in relation to all the others and the two generations also are, reciprocally, performers and observers. It is the total interconnectedness that gives the *foyer* its strength and stability and protects the security of each member.

Husband and Wife

Husband and wife complement each other in their care for the well-being of the *foyer*. In *un ménage très uni* (a united household), their activities are so divided that each undertakes responsibilities that give satisfaction to both in their fulfillment. Sometimes sharing different aspects of the same task, sometimes acting independently of each other, their mutual awareness and enjoyment of each other's capabilities provide a model of interaction for the children who are their responsibility and their audience.

The husband is the provider of the money (or raw materials) on which the *foyer* depends. The wife, in turn, should look out for the sustenance of the *foyer* by using the means provided to the best advantage. This complementary relationship is not altered by the fact that working class and petit bourgeois women may work outside the home for many years after marriage, or that, nowadays, middle class men may "help" in the home. For working women, training in some skill may replace the dowry traditionally brought to a middle or upper class marriage.[19]

Dependability of income is regarded as more important than an ever-rising gradient; as far as his *foyer* is concerned, a man is regarded as successful if he can comfortably maintain his family at a level that is more or less fixed throughout his lifetime. For instance, a professional man, who has risen socially, says:

> My father had *une situation* [as a minor civil servant]. My father-in-law had *un emploi*. There is all the difference in the world between *une situation* and *un emploi*. With the *situation* one has regular wages and contributes to a pension *(verse pour une retraite),* and that made the superiority of my father. My mother-in-law often reproaches me for not having *une situation,* although I earn five or six times more than my colleagues. But rather than have larger irregular sums, they would prefer the regular salary coming at the end of each month which leads to a pension. I am considered an adventurer – and that is true – because at fifty years I ought to be approaching retirement *(la retraite)* instead of beginning my life …

The domestic economy, the running of the *ménage,* the preparation of meals in all detail, are the responsibility of the wife. In households where the income is small, the wife has the immediate responsibility for handling the largest share of it; where the income is large, she is responsible for that part assigned to the household by the husband, who need not discuss his handling of the rest. The wife is accountable for the use which she makes of money; if she does better than she is expected to do, this is to her advantage. A wife "hates to *ask* her husband for money." She hopes, rather, to be able to lay aside small sums for her own use, so as to avoid unnecessary discussions. A good housewife is one who can be counted on to make the most of the least, and all without visible effort. Discussing women's sense of economy and housewifely skills, a man praises one woman's ability to make a meal "out of nothing":"[20]

> My mother-in-law is sixty-six years old and makes the most wonderful meals *(des repas succulants)* out of nothing. She is an amazing woman. I stopped with her one month under the conditions of semi-starvation in Paris today [1947], and she fed us so well that we had *la rnaladie de foie.* She could make a feast in the desert.

The "delights of the table" – good food and good conversation – are a symbol of the combined skills and capacity for enjoyment of the husband and wife.

It is the husband's obligation to make the major and final decisions that will protect and enhance the well-being of the *foyer.* It is felt that authority is safely vested in the husband because the natural emotions he feels towards his wife and children, as well as his self-regard, will ensure the proper use of authority. Paternal authority is associated with a certain aloofness, but also with tenderness. A man may be taciturn or irritable, subject to moods or easily angered, and so on, but unless he is governed by such unsuitable emotions (in which case he might be regarded as quite unnatural – a tyrant rather than a father), it is assumed that his decisions are based on affection and reasoned experience. In the *foyer,* authority in hands other than those of the father is potentially dangerous to the whole family; in the wife's hands, because she has not been trained to carry it out; in the children's hands, because it interferes with the expression of respect and gratitude, the reciprocals of tenderness. The husband, however, "listens to his wife's advice."

Comparing the position of husband and wife in France and America, a man comments:

> The woman [in France] plays a much greater role than here. Here the husbands light their wives' cigarettes, raise their hats in elevators, but in France the husband takes his wife's advice in all important things … The husband is king, but he always asks the advice of his wife and takes this advice in the *foyer* and in business …

Reciprocally, a woman (in another interview) says:

> What is really different in America and France is the role of the husband. Here in America, the husband orders the coal [etc.] … When he comes home from work, the wife tells him about all the things that need to be done … and he attends to this. In France, the wife does all this attending to repairs, and so on. She would not think of bothering her husband about such details. She would only ask him whether he gave his permission for such and such a thing to be done at such a price. He told how much money could be spent … In France, the husband is king, you know that, don't you? His business affairs preoccupy him. When he comes home at night, the children must be kept quiet and he must not be annoyed with details … But in spite of the rôle of the king … the French wife has much more power in her home than does the American woman, in spite of all the talk to the contrary …

The wife, on the other hand, provides the "warmth" of the *foyer;* it is she who gives the *foyer* its atmosphere *(esprit).* Her place in the *foyer* is the more intimate one. For even though the husband is concerned and consulted, and has the deciding voice, it is the wife who gets things done. In her combined role of wife and mother, she stands in an intermediary position between husband and children – interpreting each to the other in terms of her greater detailed knowledge of both. It is her responsibility as a wife to build up and preserve the image of the father in the eyes of the children. She should back up publicly her husband's decisions and should maintain before the rest of the family and the world the picture of her husband as a decisive figure. At the same time, the mother interprets the children to the father, taking upon herself the responsibility for day-to-day decisions and for the small cares and worries of their upbringing. If she is successful, she is closer to the children, but the father can safely maintain the more distant but nurturing and protective position of good authority.

A man when he marries is expected to be sexually experienced so that he may skillfully and safely initiate his young wife as his sexual partner. The bachelor, through casual affairs with older, experienced women as well as through the somewhat boastful discussions which he has with age-mates and slightly older friends, is expected to have learned how to take the initiative and how to please a woman. So, a young man explains:

> Young boys always sleep with older women. This is how they learn things. They in turn teach younger and inexperienced women. This is the way sexual knowledge is transmitted. How can you do otherwise? The trouble with Americans is that they always sleep with women of their own age and never learn anything …

Traditionally, the *jeune fille* (the young, unmarried girl) was completely protected from sexual experience before marriage. She was taught to be charming and attractive and then was supposed to be guarded by the complete reserve of all those around her. Sexual matters were not referred to in the presence of a *jeune fille*. As one young bride said: "One day I was a *jeune fille;* I never heard anything. The next day I was married; it was completely changed." The young girl, women say, did not find out about "such things" from adults, not even from the mother. "There is a lot of *pudeur* (modesty) between mother and daughter in France," a woman explains. The girl learned from the occasional confidences of her slightly older married friends, from brothers, from medical students, etc. What she knew, she kept to herself. Speaking of the sexual education of the girl, a mother says:

> Here in America one speaks about sexual matters as of cabbages and turnips. That is not right either. And one should not learn about these things in the family. That would deform the spirit of the family and the mother could no longer demand respect from her children …

In the French view, a young woman's full beauty and charm must be evoked; she comes into bloom after marriage. This is perhaps symbolized in the following description of how a young husband taught his wife to appreciate champagne, told by the wife as an older woman:[21]

> It was at a magnificent party to celebrate my engagement to Jacques ... Jacques proposed a toast and poured for me my very first true French champagne
>
> At home I had sipped sparkling wines, but not the high wine that he placed before me. I brought the glass slowly to my lips, hesitated expectantly, and then swallowed. Jacques was intently watching, waiting for me to smile in pleasure – frankly, I had to force it a little, because I honestly thought it was too dry. His expression changed to one of such keen disappointment. He made up his mind that night that his wife must learn to *appreciate* champagne.
>
> In the months and years that followed, he would serve me more and more, the finest vintages that he produced. I learned the reason why Frenchmen for centuries had loved its taste. How pleased he was to see me at last *enjoy* it ...

Nowadays, the *jeune fille* is less obviously protected against the possibility of sexual experience before marriage; she goes about much more freely and has far more social experience with young men of her own generation. But, as one young woman said:

> I never had any dates with boys, at least not alone. Can you imagine that I left France at the age of twenty-three, that is, seven years ago, and until that time I went out with a boy alone perhaps three or four times. In France you don't go out on dates. Oh, I used to see young men, but always in a group, and mostly my brother's friends ...

And a young man with a university background, who has been recounting a series of early love affairs, commented:

> Until the age of twenty-four any pretty girl would do ... Now, of course, I wouldn't go to bed with any woman. Now before I start an affair I would like to be sure that she is the kind of girl I could marry without regrets, in case she became pregnant ...

That is, as the young man gains in experience, he begins to adopt towards a girl the protective *attitude* a man is supposed to have towards a prospective wife.

For a man, the charm of a mature woman is that she is "inviting"; she acts with *finesse*. As one man put it:

> We French don't like a woman to ask. The trick for our women is so to manipulate things as to obtain things from men without asking for them, so as to give a man the impression that he bestows favors without being asked for them.

At the same time, in his relationship to a woman, especially his sexual relationship, "the most important thing is to satisfy the woman. Otherwise the man has no pleasure."

A woman's life, even today when she may have a job or a profession, is expected to center on her *foyer*. Commenting on the relative independence of American and French women, a woman says:

> Lots of French women work, but they come home in the evening. It is very uncommon for women to go out with their own friends [in the evenings]. Husbands don't like the wives to go out alone …

That is, a woman may have interests outside her home – work, friends, charities, and so on – but her activities away from the *foyer* are less formalized than the man's, or than the American woman's are thought of as being (i. e., "French women don't belong to clubs … "). Nothing that she does outside the home should interfere with her position in the *foyer* or detract from the husband's feeling of exclusive possession.

The man, in contrast, lives a more formally segmented life and is expected to have a variety of interests outside the *foyer* that do not touch upon it in any way. If the husband does not thereby deprive the *foyer* materially, it is not considered impermissible for him to have a mistress; he is, however, expected to maintain and protect his wife's exclusive position within the *foyer* as *mère de mes enfants* (mother of my children).[22] In cases of marital infidelity, the actual participant is expected to keep them to himself; anyone else – in the *foyer* or in a protective relationship to it – who finds out or suspects should keep silent. Only by so doing does the man protect his own position and dignity; and others, the peaceful continuance and privacy of the *foyer*.

Father and Children

The father in his responsible role stands slightly apart from everyday events and problems in the *foyer*. Children are taught to be quiet when father comes home so as not to disturb his repose. They are expected to accept his decisions with good grace: *"Pas de discussions, pas de drames"* (no discussions, no scenes) is a remembered admonition. Speaking of the father, in comparison to the mother, the comment is made: *"Il ne s'occupait pas de nous"* (he had no time for us), even though the father is very much present in the home. The father, unlike the mother, keeps order by an implicit distantiation in his behavior and attitudes. This is particularly the case when the children are very young; then, though he may play with them occasionally, he has little to do with their intimate care. Only when the children are older does the father begin to have a private relationship to his children – through his concern for the education *(formation)* of his son, through his response to the developing charm of his daughter.

French children early learn of the existence – somewhere vaguely outside the *foyer* – of a sinister male mythological figure, to which is attributed excessive violence, destructive sexuality, and other aggressive characteristics. This bogey has various names and appearances: *loup-garou, Ramponneau, lustucru, croque-mitaine, le satyre,* etc.; the names and stories of sadistic murderers may also be associated with him; or, even more vaguely, "the black man," or "the gypsies," or "the gendarmes," etc. Lullabies sung to the child tell of the bogey who would come to carry off

> *tous les petits gars*
> *qui ne dorment pas ...*

Sometimes the bogey is invoked as an alternative to the punishing father, as when a man recalled that

> his mother would threaten him if he did not go to sleep at night – sometimes by having his father come upstairs, other times the threat was of the *croque-mitaine ...*

Mothers tell their daughters (at ten or twelve years) to beware of "strangers" or to "walk straight ahead and look neither to the right nor to the left" when they go out of the house alone to school or on errands; women remember stories about vicious murderers discussed in their presence by adults or told them as cautionary tales. As men and women recall them, the stories of these bogeys were told them by women (mother, grandmother, nurse, servant); their existence was scoffed at by men. So, for instance, a young woman said that her father had told her "these stories are old-fashioned; nobody believes them anymore." She then went on to describe how her nurse had told her stories about Pantagruel. Belief in the imminence of the *monstre* disappears as the child begins to move further out into the everyday world. Dispelled from reality, the bogey recurs in fantasies about the dangers of the world outside the bounds of usual experience. Speaking about the child's imagination (when it is four or five years old), a young man comments that

> ... fairy stories are preferable to all these gangster stories, the comics you have here. Here [in the United States] one plunges the child into reality. Why throw the child into reality? ... the child has need of a certain sum of dreams ... [And later, on the same subject:] The story has a great influence ... It concerns a world built beyond reality. More than here – these stories of Tarzan, of gangsters – these are too near to us ...[23]

These fantasy figures of bogeys are available as recipients of the negative feelings and fears that the very young child might otherwise direct onto the image of the father, particularly in his night-time role. It would seem, then, that the image of the male is split: on the one hand, into a dangerous figure, but one from which the child – within the *foyer* – is safe as it is envisaged as existing somewhere outside the *foyer*; on the other hand, into a succoring, protective, and undestructive figure that is the father within the *foyer* in his relationship to son and daughter.

Father and son

The father's main duty is to supervise and assist in the education and development of his son, teaching and facilitating the acquisition of those skills on which the achievement of adulthood depends. This facilitation includes permissiveness towards his adolescent son's sexual education. Actually, an uncle or some other man who is an intimate friend of the father may take over some of the more permissive and indulgent aspects of the father; the father condones, without becoming involved in, this phase of his son's development. Women think of father and son being more open than mother and daughter; men, however, say that they did not discuss sexual questions with their father.[24]

The relationship between father and young son can be an exceedingly tender one, in which the father – when the boy is old enough to be released from his mother – literally or figuratively takes his son on brief excursions outside the *foyer* into a man's world of interests, though as a guide rather than as a companion.[25] Yet it is striking that, as an adult, the son's memory image of his father is not that of someone close, but rather distant, even "cold." The father does not attempt to enter the son's world as an older "friend" or "comrade"; he remains reserved and his son "respects" him. Thus, a young man says:

> My father has always been a very reserved person ... We often had discussions of ideas and opinions with my father, but never anything personal. I respect him because his life has been so straight and honest ...

In late adolescence, the boy begins to break away from the parental *foyer*. This appears to be experienced by the boy as a need to have a personality of his own, to act on his own initiative. Speaking of this period, a young man says:

> ... [the child] assimilates what the adults are saying. At the age of eighteen or twenty in France, he can have opinions which are entirely personal. It requires much personal initiative. It is necessary [then] to insist upon personal initiative ...

And another young man, who has been describing his efforts to work out a career in terms of his personal preferences, comments:

> The French are always looking for order in their own lives, for a style of living which corresponds to the ideas one has of life …

Thus, the desire to have a life and opinions of one's own is experienced not as an act of antagonism against a person (e. g., the father), but rather as a response to a system of tutelage. Speaking of this, the young man says:

> Just at eighteen or twenty years I was suffocated *(étouffé)*. I discovered a personality for myself at the moment when I was liberated from my studies [in the lycée].

This insistence upon "personal initiative" and upon the search for a personally defined "style of living" does not precede, but follows on the boy's main education; that is, the demand develops out of learning based on earlier decisions by the parents, especially the father.

In his supervisory role, it is the father's duty to foresee and prepare his son for this situation, so that the young man in his turn will be able to live in an independent *foyer*. For it is certain that the ability to establish and maintain a *foyer* – actual or symbolic – is for the French the measure of the man. The emphasis on the father's superior knowledge and skill puts the onus for avoiding father-son rivalry on the father. It is possible, then, that the son's memory of the father as "cold" and "reserved" reflects his sense of the father's partial withdrawal during a period of difficult transition. Although in recall the father appears to be somewhat unapproachable, he remains a man whom the son can safely emulate in his own way.

Yet rivalry between father and son provides one of the major themes in contemporary French films.[26] In films in which this problem is explored, a common situation is that of a father-figure and a son-figure both in love with a beautiful young woman (a daughter-figure or one who resembles the young mature woman). The woman may return the love of one or the other of the men (often she is seen first in a relationship to the elder and later to the younger of them – but the order may be reversed); in the end, she may disappoint both men. In these representations, the focus of sympathy and attention is, as a rule, the elder man and, even when he is not the central character, the dramatic possibilities of the plot develop out of his ability to make the climax-producing decisions. His power of attraction may be superior to that of the younger man or, on the contrary, his realization of his waning attractiveness may be a source of pathos and, possibly, tragedy – he has the power to obstruct the young man's happiness but not to achieve his own. It rests with him whether to assert his strength or to withdraw and still prevent the young couple from being united or to withdraw and use his power of decision to bring them together. Thus, while in such situations one or the other of the men suffers a love disappointment (and sometimes both do), the focus is likely to be upon the struggle of the elder man who, even when he turns out to be evil (e. g., the elderly husband in *Le Corbeau*) or is publicly misjudged and victimized (e. g. the elderly man in *Panique*), remains a sympathetic or a pitiable but still dignified personality. In the role of the elderly lover of a young woman, the two images of the adult male – the authoritative and nurturing father within the *foyer* and the dangerous stranger outside the *foyer* – appear to be fused. In this adult version the "dangerous" figure (as envisaged in the childhood bogey), although a threat to the young man, is also understood to be a suffering human being. As Martha Wolfenstein and Nathan Leites have pointed out: "The effort of French films to reconcile discrepant aspects of the father seems to express a preoccupation with the father image which extends into the mature life of the son. The real-life father presumably remains a person of importance for his grown-up son. As the relation continues to be a present emotional reality, the son tends to bring to his understanding of his father his own later experience in becoming a lover and a father and in facing the prospect of growing old. Accordingly, childhood impressions of the father become transformed; the father image continues to develop and formerly irreconcilable elements tend to merge."[27]

In these fantasy treatments of father-son rivalry, even though the son is threatened by the father, the father remains an accessible figure with whom identification remains possible.

Father and daughter

The daughter potentially presents the greatest gratification and the greatest temptation to the father. For the daughter, the father is a protective, unfrightening, sexually attractive figure. She learns early that the father can be cajoled by appropriate behavior into kindnesses and concessions that might not otherwise be forthcoming. From adolescence and even earlier the feminine qualities of the daughter who is pretty, *caline* (coaxing, caressing), and *chic,* are a source of enjoyment to the father and he will respond to her in a playfully courting manner.

Speaking of familial relations, a daughter says:

> A father has a tendency to consider his daughter as something very perfect and attributes to her all the virtues that his wife does not have in his eyes.

> There is a tie of friendship and *camaraderie* that is lacking between him and his wife ... [And later, returning to the same subject] When a daughter misbehaves, the father often takes it as a personal offense. It is as if she were unfaithful to her father. In that case, the father can be terrible ...

And an older married couple, in a joint interview, describe the relationship of father and daughter:

> *Husband:* ... He is proud of her and treats her *cornme une petite aimée* (like a little sweetheart) ...
> *Wife:* There is *grande amitié* (great friendship) between fathers and daughters.

Here it is worth noting the wife's subtle and certainly unintentional modification of the husband's phrase. Later in the same interview, the man describes a father-daughter relationship about which "you would have said they were *amant et maîtresse* (lover and mistress), there was so much tenderness." He himself then commented: *"(Ça ne sortait pas des limites de bienséance"* (it doesn't go beyond the limits of propriety).

In the relationship between father and daughter there is much more open expression of feeling than between father and son: daughters speak of quarrels and disagreements with their father as well as about their affection and admiration for him, even though they too refer to the father's strictness and aloofness. It is as if greater freedom in the expression of feeling were possible between father and daughter because, inevitably, the daughter will leave the *foyer*.

Traditionally, the father provided the daughter with a *dot* (dowry); nowadays he is more likely to see that she is educated so that she has a *métier* or profession that will give her a certain security and also add to her attractiveness as a prospective wife. In this way the father has a deciding voice in arrangements for his daughter's future, though not necessarily in the selection of a husband.

The daughter is likely to seek as a husband a man embodying at least some of the qualities of the father. Disparity of age is not considered to provide an unfavorable prognosis for marriage.

Mother and Children

The mother takes complete care of the infant and very small child. She makes most of the day-to-day decisions about the child and also sees to it that the father's decisions are carried out. The imposing of discipline is the mother's task and an undisciplined child is a reproach to the mother. It is through its relationship to the mother that the child learns how to become responsive; the child's failure to respond and its errors in response reflect upon the mother's affection and ability to teach.

In contrast to the split image of the father, there is no separate female image toward which negative or hostile feelings about the mother may be directed. The mother is viewed with more openly expressed ambivalence than the father, for, as well as the source of the chief gratifications of childhood, she is the source of the chief restrictions. The French quite consistently conceptualize external figures of authority (Justice, the Censorship, even France herself) as feminine. Behind the figure of the king with his absolute power, there is the figure of the woman who (without asking) gives him advice and influences him – and who, in turn, may be influenced by others.[28]

Unlike the image of the lovable man, who grows in stature and importance with age and experience, the image of the lovable woman – whatever her age – is accorded qualities of grace and attractiveness that are especially those of the young mature woman. A woman's charm depends not upon the cultivation of "youthfulness" as such, but of qualities which are especially those of the young woman yet grace her at any age. It is precisely these qualities which a disappointed bitter woman lacks, but which, in courtesy, are accorded the old woman who has been beautiful.

Mother and son

The mother takes pride in her son's skills and successes in all fields. She prepares him to become an adult and to achieve success by the most scrupulous attention to his education and training and by resisting the temptation to spoil him by over-indulgence. The mother buys (or has made or makes) the boy's clothes. It is she who, in the first instance, reads his school reports and who goes to school when there is trouble (*"jamais le père"* – never the father – informants say); it is she – in the family – who waits with open trepidation when he takes examinations. The mother slaps and spanks, and also smiles when all goes well.

The mother may threaten to tell the father about disobedience – and sometimes does, for he takes over more serious problems; but the mother also defends the boy before the father.

The mother's tenderness towards her adolescent son may not be exhibited to the same degree as that of the father towards his daughter; the son's behavior towards the mother should always be modified by the respect and obedience which he owes her. Young men are likely to receive their sexual training from women of the mother's generation, women who – whether of the same or of a different social class – are somewhat maternal towards them. The mother may be aware of the son's sexual adventures; indeed, she may take pride in his success; however, respect for the mother includes keeping from her definite knowledge of the son's casual affairs. This the father will enforce. Thus, an informant describes how a father called his son to his office and reprimanded him for returning from a night with his mistress only at breakfast time – such carelessness, the father said, showed "lack of respect for the mother."

The mother may make something of a companion of her growing son. She may even, when he is adolescent, confide in him and look to him for advice and solace. She does not, however, expect the boy to side with her openly against the father and, indeed, may repudiate his offers of assistance if the father's position is thereby called into question. When she makes the son aware of the father's weaknesses and failures, she continues to support the father's nominal position. Thus, both husband-wife and father-son relationships are positively supported by the mother in the eyes of the son; the crossing of the lines of dyadic relationships does not endanger their existence when there is no public acknowledgment of the fact.

The mother has a deciding voice in her son's marriage; she may regard it as a distinct sacrifice when he marries a woman of his but not of her choosing. A mother may expect to have some continuing voice in her son's *foyer*.

Though she makes heavy demands upon her son, the mother – in contrast to the father – is in the son's eyes the one who knows without being told, who is intuitive and responsive in her understanding. Describing his parents, a young man writes:

> My mother, on the contrary, was entirely intuitive. She was one of those women who understand with fairness, without heeding to reason: to her everything seemed to be natural, indeed, even familiar.

Mother and daughter

The mother is the teacher and disciplinarian of the daughter as well as of the son and should equip the daughter with all the arts and skills she possesses; by doing so, she equips a rival capable, in a sense, of displacing her. French mothers tend to insist on the daughter's immaturity as long as possible; daughters rely on the mother for training and on her judgment of their adequacy, and tend to acquiesce in the situation. But the need to prove to herself (and possibly to the mother?) her developing femininity and skill seems to be a factor in the daughter's turning to the father for favor and appreciation. This may serve only to increase existing tensions between mother and daughter.

A major demand made by the French daughter upon her mother is not that the mother should be lenient, but that she should be *juste* (exact, fair) – not showing favoritism, not acting capriciously, but fol-

lowing a consistent and understandable line in the exercise of authority. So, a young mother says of her own upbringing

> that she sees now for the first time what was good in the upbringing of
> French children. Her mother brought her up strictly but [was] very *juste*.
> She did not always feel that her mother had been *juste,* but now she sees
> that she was. In America mothers are less strict, but not so *juste*. They
> leave a girl with feelings of uncertainty …

The mother's lack of fairness is likely to be demonstrated by her
attempts to delay her daughter's adoption of an adult role: dressing
her like a child, refusing to allow her to wear make-up, censoring her
reading, and generally keeping her unself-confident. As *daughters,*
French women complain that they learned little or nothing about
their sexual role at home; as *mothers* they explain that discussion of
such a subject is not possible at home *entre proches* (between closely
related persons, meaning here mother and daughter).[29]

Traditionally, the mother arranges the daughter's marriage. In the
case of a daughter who is a too attractive rival, this is likely to take
place early. Though theoretically a married woman should be completely self-sufficient in managing her *foyer,* a young married daughter is likely to return to her mother for advice, rather than look to
outsiders or to professional sources of information.[30] In this way the
mother may have a continuing voice in her daughter's adult life. It is
at this time, apparently, that the daughter recognizes that, after all,
her own mother was *juste*. As one older woman said:

> Once the daughter is married, you know, the relationship [between
> mother and daughter] changes. There is much more physical intimacy
> *(intimité physique)*. After marriage there is equality.

Siblings

Brothers

In early childhood and usually through adolescence, the relationship
of brothers who are near in age is friendly and companionable and
without overt rivalry. Young brothers are likely to spend much of
their time together and, although their personal interests and school
friendships may lead them in different directions, they are apt to keep
a certain solidarity and to support each other mutually against adults
and unwelcome outsiders of their own age. Recollecting his comradeship with a slightly older brother, a man says:

> I was very close to my brother; you know, the fact that we went through school always in the same grade, and we always ganged up together against my parents *(faisaient équipe contre les parents)*. We fought a lot with other boys. We always covered for each other in front of the parents. But we were also always punished together. For minor mischief and pranks … by my mother, for major ones by my father … Personally, I think that punishing the guilty and the innocent jointly is a very good principle. It develops the *esprit de corps*.

When brothers are far apart in age, there may be little intimate contact between them; sometimes the relationship may be closer to that of father and son with the much older brother taking over some of the more permissive characteristics of the father.

The friendly relationship between brothers appears to become somewhat attenuated after adolescence, perhaps to avoid situations of rivalry. Frenchmen seem to participate less in the sexual or business lives of their brothers (except when both are involved in a family business), than they may in those of associates and friends. On this point an informant comments:

> It is a curious thing that in spite of the close ties and great friendship that existed between me and my brother, he never took me into his confidence [about his activities in the Resistance], never told me exactly what he was doing … I don't think he did it because of the nature of his work. He just did not confide in me …

And again:

> Strangely enough, considering the friendship with my brother, I know nothing about his sentimental life. I learned about sex from other boys and nothing from my brother …

The warm feeling of *fraternité* is, however, highly valued and provides a basis for other relationships developed in late adolescence and in adult life. Women no less than men appreciate the importance men attribute to masculine friendships and the profound loyalty one man may have for another The basis for the understanding of masculine friendship appears to be built up in the *foyer*.[31]

Sisters

In contrast to brothers, sisters are likely to be regarded as competitors. In the *foyer* this is the relationship in which hostility is most readily permitted to come to the surface. Sisters, like brothers, are expected to share some of their possessions and they may spend a great deal of time together. Speaking about each other, however, they are more likely to emphasize their differences than what they have in common. A girl, for instance, so describes her sister:

> She is older, two years older ... So we never did anything together. We had one room but we never did anything together ... We are completely different. My sister always wanted to do things the right way, I was the rebel ... [And later, returning to the same topic:] But my sister is completely different from me. We used to call her *la fille de Hollywood*. She was completely American ...

Sisters may complain that the mother is not *juste* (fair) in her treatment of them, or that the father shows favoritism towards one or the other. Criticisms not otherwise expressed come out or are implied in statements by and about sisters, i.e., "She [an elder sister, also much admired] was completely cold"; or "She [a younger sister, the baby who was spoiled by the whole family] is entirely too strict with her boys"; or "She [a sister said to be preferred by the father] goes around for days not saying anything"; and so on. Apparently, as between sisters, statements of difference – not always involving an invidious comparison – are ways both of expressing and of handling hostility. For sisters also expect the differences between them to be recognized and respected by their parents – they expect to be treated fairly, but not alike.

During adolescence, sisters may be in open competition for the father's attention and regard, not copying each other but rather trying in different ways to appeal to the father's interest. So, in one family one sister wanted to become an artist like her father (and later married an artist whom her father liked), while another sister tried to become a perfect housewife (an occupation despised by the first), and so on. As each sister seeks a distinctive style, each accentuates but also modifies the competition between them.

Vindictive elder and ill-treated younger sisters are constant figures in French folk-tales. In contemporary film treatment of sisterly relations, hostility is likely to be expressed as envy: the disappointed elder sister envying what she has lost or has never had, the precocious younger sister envying what she is not yet ready for. [32]

Except when sisters are in a semimaternal and protective relationship to younger siblings (brothers as well as sisters), the French do not appear to have formal ways of describing the warm devotion that, quite apparently, does exist between sisters; like the more intimate aspects of other relationships the less clearly verbalized aspects of sisters' feelings for each other appear to be difficult to discuss with outsiders.

Brother and sister

As children, near-age brother and sister are on terms of casual physical intimacy and candor little touched by shyness. While they are still quite young, children from different *foyers* may play together, but during the school years there is a formal separation of boys and girls outside the *foyer*. Then it is mainly through sister or brother (or perhaps cousin) that the child has glimpses of a world of activities apart from its own. ("I don't know about girls," a man comments, "I never had a sister.") During these years when age-mates of the same sex are bound by a strong *esprit de corps,* brother and sister remain in affectionate relationship to each other.

Children are given little responsibility for one another, but there is a mutual protectiveness between brother and sister, its form depending somewhat on which is the elder. For instance, speaking of childhood quarrels, a woman describes the "only" occasion on which she

> got really mad at her elder brother and started to attack him physically. He turned his back and she pummeled him hard. He just stood there and waited for her to stop. A brother would never fight his sister. With her younger brother, she does not believe she would have done such a thing. He was younger and had to be protected.

Between adolescence and marriage, the sister relies on and confides in her brother; her pleasures and freedom depend to some extent on his willingness and acquiescence. For, unless there is much disparity in age, the adolescent brother will act as protector and escort to his sister when she goes out of the *foyer*. The brother may also make a partial *confidente* of his sister and she may shield him before the parents. In this there is an important difference between brothers and brother and sister, in that boys form a kind of team in which each helps the other to conceal like activities, while a brother depends upon his sister to keep secret activities in which she has no part and of which she may have no detailed knowledge.

The older brother is responsible for the safety and virginity of his sister; this is normally the first adult responsibility placed on a young Frenchman. The brother will introduce to his sister suitable young men – not necessarily from among his closest friends – among whom she may find a husband. Similarly, a sister introduces to the brother girls among whom he may find a wife or possibly even a mistress. Nowadays there is some merging, as they grow older, of the adolescent groups of brother's and sister's friends; in attenuated form these mixed groups without explicit courtship behavior continue the casual, noncourting but dependable relations of brother and sister.

When there is a wide disparity in age, brother and sister – if at all intimate – may have a relationship closer to that of parent and child. If there is no actual *foyer* to which the pair belong, as may happen in the case of orphans, such a pseudo-parent child relationship may be deeply valued as a partial, but rather pathetic, substitute for a total *foyer*.

The relationship between brother and sister, when it rests upon an experience of mutual dependability though not necessarily upon adult congeniality, appears to be the most stable and enduring within the parental *foyer* and the family of near relatives.[33]

II. EDUCATION: THE CHILD IN THE FOYER

French childhood is a long apprenticeship in becoming a person. Through training, the child gradually is transformed from a small being (*un petit être*) into an individual, an adult with an awakened spirit, a developed imagination, and a critical intelligence, who knows the behavior appropriate to a man and a woman, and who has acquired the skills and control necessary for well-being. The disciplines imposed on the child by its parents and later by teachers and others responsible for its training, are oriented towards its adequacy in adulthood; the experiences of childhood are conceived of as necessary preparations rather than as pleasant in themselves. Retrospectively, however, the incessant *devoirs* (lessons, duties) and disciplines associated with childhood are valued as they have helped one to become a person, to avoid – or at least minimize – *malheur* and to achieve *bonheur.*

In the French view, all activities have inherent in them potentialities for *bonheur* and *malheur.* Neither of these terms is readily translatable into English; *bonheur* carries combined meanings of welfare, felicity, good fortune, etc., but with implications not in any one of these terms. Only through trained knowledge can one know what the potentialities for *bonheur* and *malheur* are; only through the exercise of skill and enlightened control can one achieve the delicate balance that is, essentially, *bonheur. Bonheur* is regarded as fragile and transitory, its attainment dependent not only upon the person's own developed capabilities, but also upon the people around him and upon circumstance. *Malheur* will follow almost inevitably upon failure to exercise skill and control, but at the same time it is not necessarily of the individual's own making.[34] Children of their own accord cannot achieve *bonheur. Le bonheur du foyer* is in the keeping of the parents and part of their responsibility in creating and maintaining it is the training of their children. To become a person, to achieve *bonheur,* education *(formation)* is indispensable.

For the French, development is a lifelong process; the individual can continue to evolve indefinitely. Full maturity comes only in later years of life; the individual is most himself when he is most highly skilled. This means, essentially, that there is no discontinuity in the learning process. Nevertheless, for the young girl, marriage, and for the young man, formal independence of the parental *foyer* – when his education and/or apprenticeship are finished – traditionally mark transitions in the development towards maturity in that both woman and man are now regarded as capable of autonomy and therefore of personal responsibility. Before this, as children in the *foyer,* they are taught good habits *(les bonnes habitudes)* and are given education *(education, formation)* and training *(instruction)* in the specific skills on which the achievement of individuality and adulthood depend. Thereafter they are able to make reasonable choices, to elaborate in their own way upon what they already are; they are "formed." Development, however, still continues. Full maturity for the man may come only after the death of the parents.

The child is regarded as human at least from the time it is born – certainly from the moment when the mother, having accepted the pain of childbirth for its sake, "forgets" the pain *(douleur)* in the happiness of holding; her child; perhaps even before, as the responsibility for having a child and caring for it adequately involves forethought and planning. Conception is believed to be more certain when the man and woman both share in the pleasure, but a couple who give way to impulse without forethought may be regarded as having "descended to the level of animals" *(descendre au niveau des animaux).* Commenting on the small French family, a young man says:

> A family of five children, that's not intelligent. That is a manifestation of animality, of backwardness. Everything must be governed *(dirigé);* it is only that way that something good can be achieved …

Another young man uses similar imagery to express instead the need for spontaneity in parents, when he says that

> … the experience of the war years has given a healthier attitude towards basic necessities and more natural and animal attitudes towards life. [People] have tended to return to the more primitive nucleus with children as the internal center of the family.

Common to these two views is the feeling that parents themselves must be fully human – spontaneous but also acting with directed thought – to ensure the welfare of the child.

Valued as a human being and for what it will become, the infant requires the constant solicitous care of its parents, especially the mother. For the infant, training must begin early and everything, even sucking, may have to be learned. The young mother, urged to breast feed her infant, may be told:[35]

> You have milk, but it is baby who is lazy *(parasseux)* …

Before the infant has been trained, it is regarded as acting mainly upon caprice. The mother is warned in a variety of contexts never to become a slave to the infant's caprices, lest it tyrannize over the parents:[36]

> The education of the child ought in effect to commence early (*de bonne heure*). One should never nag a child, it makes it fidget, one should never hit it, but one ought to know not to accede to its caprices. One must give it regular habits, not admit that it can refuse …

Even where the much older child is concerned, dislike of some article of clothing, or an expressed preference for a career, and so on, may be disregarded because the child is thought to be motivated by mere "caprice" – by fantasy. As everything must be learned and as the infant is incapable of giving adequate clues to its needs and may not even, at first, be able to respond correctly to clues given by the mother, it is assumed that the mother must exercise her own judgment and set the pace for the infant.

The infant, especially the newborn infant, is considered to be extremely fragile and endangered in various ways by a possibly hostile environment, from which its parents must vigilantly protect it. The mother may be warned:[37]

> The newborn infant (*le nouveau-né*) is a little being unfortunately very badly adapted to external life (*à la vie extérieure*); while all little animals are, from their first hours, able to live by themselves, the human child (*le petit d'homme*) must vie with (*lutter*) a series of dangers which threaten it; it only adapts itself very gradually to the exterior life (*il ne s'adopte que très progressivement à la vie extérieure*).

These menacing dangers – cold, drafts, germs, and so on – are placed in the external world, mainly in the material environment, and they must be warded off by careful parents who bring about the infant's gradual adaptation. It is the adult human environment that is determining.

The character and behavior of the parents determine those of the child. So, for instance, one author describes the "nervous child," i.e., the child who cries and makes scenes:[38]

> In reality, these are very often children brought up by nervous persons and furthermore they are habitually children badly brought up (*mal élevé*) to whom one has made concessions rather than troubling oneself with their scenes. Very young the baby perceives that it suffices to cry or to put itself into a temper (*se mettre en colère*) to make its parents concede. No medicine can replace education …

Later, describing the healthy child brought up by good parents, the same author writes:[39]

An infant well brought up and well cared for *(bien élevé et bien soigné)* is gay and smiling; later he will become an adult who is well and happy *(bien portant et heureux)*.

The conception of the determinative effect of parental character and training upon the character of the child appears to be an exceedingly stable one in French culture. It was, for instance, a recurrent theme one hundred fifty years ago in the discussions of the *Conseil d'Etat* regarding proposed laws concerning the family in the Civil Code. Commenting on proposed controls of paternal authority, a speaker said:[40]

> Generally the mistakes of the children are the result of the weaknesses, the thoughtlessness, or the bad examples of the fathers; therefore these do not deserve absolute confidence ...

The similarity of attitudes in recent discussions about reforms in the Civil Code is very striking.[41]

Some contemporary French child care manuals recommend a more or less "hands off" policy in the education of the young infant (reminiscent in certain respects of a passing American fashion). Specifically, certain recommended practices are in contrast to traditional forms of French child rearing – as these traditional practices have been described by informants and observers. For instance, contrary to what is recommended, there is said to be almost continuous warm, emotional interaction between mother and infant and small child during its waking hours. During early childhood, it is the father who remains the more distant figure.[42] But, different as recommendation and practice may be in detail, common to both is the assumption that parents initiate and stimulate, while children learn through response, not through exploration and experiment.

A common image of parent and child in their educational relationship is that of the gardener and the plant which he is cultivating. So, the author of a child care manual writes:[43]

> The child is a delicate plant, very delicate, and on its first year depends the health *(santé)* of its whole life ...

Similarly, another author writes:[44]

> The craft *(métier)* of parents is not the same as another, for we have seen it has not to do with forming a child according to uniform methods. Some good observers have said that the *métier* of parents is not that of a worker who makes *(fabrique)* an object according to a model, but that of a gardener who, knowing the needs of each species, assures to his trees the earth, the space necessary to their proper development, seeking how-

ever by appropriate means to make disappear useless branches and thus to increase their vigor. It is, in fact, a *métier* even more delicate. For all the trees of one species flower together, while children of the same age do not have the same possibilities. It is, then, each particular case which one must know.

These nurturing garden images recall two others, i.e., *faire souche* (to graft – *souche* is literally the stump of the tree left in the ground when the tree is felled and metaphorically the understock on which is grafted the fruit to be cultivated) which, figuratively, means to found a family and so to take root; and its opposite, *déraciné* (uprooted) which, figuratively, may be used to refer to anyone away from his own *milieu* (e. g., "a provincial going to Paris is a *déraciné*"). So, metaphorically, the individual is likened to a cultivated fruit tree – grafted, pruned, and trained to produce as much fruit as is consonant with its taking up an appropriate portion of the limited garden space.[45] And ideally the orchard contains a variety of trees within a small space, the optimum size of each tree being calculated from the moment of first grafting.[46] So too each individual is trained to realize his unique potentialities within the limits set by the *foyer* in which he is reared.

　　As the image of the gardener and the tree suggests, it is the role of parents as educators to know and decide, to protect and initiate, to train and correct – in a word, to "form" the child. Knowing "each particular case," the parents can recognize each child's potential talents and special needs. On the other hand, it is the role of the child, as learner, to respond and accept correction and so grow into an acceptable individual. This conception of child rearing is implied in French comments about American parents and children and in comparisons of French and American training. So, a French teacher criticizes her American pupils:

> American children enjoy too much liberty and independence. A child should fear his elders, otherwise he has no respect and becomes wild …

Or a young man compares the effects of early freedom of choice on American and French children:

> Formation is indispensable. If the child were left to himself, one would be making a misfit (*on en ferait un raté*) … Here boys of twelve express themselves better than do those of eighteen in France. That can be very dangerous, that bungles gifts (*ça gache les dons*) …

Or a French girl compares the handling of an American child with her own education:

That child has not received any moral basis for action from her parents [American]. While [my] parents were always telling me what to do, at the same time they tried to develop my own judgment and good sense. This education is much better than giving complete liberty to children …

Ideally, parents are regarded as positively motivated and as acting positively in their educative role, whether they are enjoining a child to behave in a certain way or are preventing it from falling victim to its own untrained impulses *(caprices)* or to the dangers to which it is exposed before it knows how to cope with them. The human environment of the child in the *foyer* is regarded not only as determining, but also as protective and succoring.

French education consists principally in instilling in the learner the habits and knowledge and skills necessary to adult life before there is occasion to put the skills to use. When the occasion does arise, the individual will then be fully prepared to meet it adequately. Understanding and pleasure in the exercise of a skill are expected to follow upon rather than to precede or accompany learning. This is related to a conception of personality development and growth as a process of unfolding potentialities, each of which alters as it is integrated into the whole.[47] The personality, as it were, goes through a series of transformations, each having potentialities for new learning. Thus, until it is about six years old, the child is believed not to be able to distinguish clearly between "truth and falsehood"; and only when it is about twelve can it begin to grasp abstract thought, and so on. French education is related also to a conception of learning as a process of continual expansion, enrichment, refinement, and clarification. This means, on the one hand, that the skeleton of the structure as a whole can be laid down early – as the potentialities for learning appear – and that, to the extent that knowledge is mastered, it is a permanent acquisition. On the other hand, it means that learning cannot be hurried, but is expected to proceed slowly until the full complement of skills has been acquired.

In educating the child, it is said, it is necessary to keep the child at its own level: *on laisse l'enfant sur son plan d'enfant, à son degré d'enfant.* That is, one should not expect the child to act (i. e., make choices, experiment) before it has learned. But each child develops at its own pace, in keeping with its abilities, and parents show their awareness of the child's qualities in the way in which they set the pace for the child. For instance, a girl, describing her parents' treatment of herself and her younger sister, explains that her sister

remained a baby much longer than C. herself, and therefore she was not permitted to do certain things and read certain books which C. could do at a much earlier age. Even the so-called 'intelligent conversations' were different when the adults were speaking to C. or to her sister.

And a mother, critical of "the American insistence on age rather than ability" in school, comments:

> That is very stupid. There are children of fourteen who have a mind *(esprit)* totally different from other children of the same age. All French mothers know that ... The mind *(esprit)* is the result of intelligence and education *(l'intelligence et l'education)* ... [Holding children back in school] is squandering *(gaspillage),* loss of time. It is bad.

The learning child, whether infant or adolescent, lives within a universe bounded by its own limitations of skill and control, as these are judged by the parents, and it is protected from dangers that may "menace" it from without and from indulgence in impulsive behavior that may either spoil its own gifts or endanger other people. Thus, because it is fragile and must be protected from cold and drafts, mothers say, the infant is dressed in several layers of clothing and, at least in the early months of life, is placed in a *maillot,* a kind of bag (sometimes a small blanket is used) which first encloses its arms but later only its torso and legs. The *maillot* does not bind but restricts the possibility of movement as it also keeps the child warm. Later, when the baby can safely sit – and has been propped against pillows – it may be placed in a baby swing (the so-called *youp-la*) to "exercise its legs" in preparation for walking. Still later, when it is already standing up, it may be put in a pen *(pare)* where it can move around in a restricted but safe space.[48] In this way the infant slowly progresses from the state in which it lies – and is carried in cradling arms – in protected semi-immobility to one in which, having gained control and skill, it moves safely within a larger area. Having learned, once able to act adequately, the particular restrictions are re-moved.

An important part of the child's education consists in awakening *(éveiller,* which also carries the meaning of "enlivening" in this context) its mind and imagination, sensitizing it to stimulation so that it may be developed. *Éveiller,* however, refers both to the process of awakening and the quality of the trained and stimulated mind: the wholesome, growing child has *unesprit éveillé.*[49] Speaking of the process by which this awakening is – achieved, a French *lycée* teacher comments:

> French education is completely different from education in America. I might even say that the whole system is completely different, and permit me to tell you that I personally prefer the French system ... The primary aim of French educators is to develop *l'esprit* and *l'indépendance et l'esprit critique.* We want our children to develop into independent

thinkers capable of making intellectual decisions. As a result, French children are much quicker than American children and have *l'esprit plus vif* (a more lively mind).

Similarly, another teacher, speaking of a kindergarten, says that

she is all for developing imagination, logic and reasoning.

She describes the children's games as

rather educational, to develop the imagination and intelligence, than physical.

This gradual awakening of the child – bringing it into awareness – seems to be perceived as a gradual clarification, a response poetically described by Pierre Loti in writing about his earliest recollections (at two to three years of age):[50]

I came forth from the darkness of unconsciousness very gradually, for my mind was illumined only fitfully, but then by outbursts of splendor that compelled and fascinated my infant gaze. When the light was extinguished, I lapsed once more into the non-consciousness of a new-born animal, of the tiny plant just germinating.

At first my mind, altogether, unimpressed and undeveloped, may be compared to a photographer's apparatus fitted with its sensitized glass. Objects insufficiently lighted up make no impression upon the virgin plates; but when a vivid splendor falls upon them, and when they are encircled by disks of light, these once dim objects now engrave themselves upon the glass. My first recollections are of bright summer days and sparkling noon times, – or more truly, are recollections of the light of wood fires burning with great ruddy flames.

Imagination and intelligence are stimulated by presenting the child with correct models, from which it learns how to direct its thought and feeling into appropriate channels. The child learns by following the models and then by making adaptations from them. The importance of models is stated unequivocally in very different contexts; for instance, in an article on "civilization," François Berge writes:[51]

For ... man tends always to become like the image which he makes of himself ... in denying the sacred which was in him, man has left nothing more than the animal. A model of man which does not distinguish him essentially from animals can make of him nothing but an ape or a wolf. And an image which does not distinguish him from a machine transforms him into a machine and dedicates him to be used without shame by the strong and the malignant.

Training the child, then, consists primarily in instruction in the rules of correct behavior, in the provision of appropriate models, and in guidance towards correct observation. Learning proceeds by rote and repetition, by absorption of the behavior of others, and by practiced response to carefully directed stimulation. It is assumed that once the rules have been learned and the examples meticulously followed, behavior will be correct and intelligible and, as it were, automatic. Elaboration can then proceed on the basis of the known.[52]

Speaking of learning, a business man says:

> Certainly we memorized and recited our lessons. I approve of it wholeheartedly. It seems to me that in that respect the French educational system is perfect. We memorize the fundamentals of education and acquire once and for all the things that are absolutely necessary later in life. In memorizing we don't have to use our intelligence and leave it free and untouched to be used later in more important things. Look at the American students. They arrive at the age of twenty not knowing anything. They don't carry anything in their heads and have to refer to dictionaries for the most insignificant information. I learned a certain amount of necessary things and will never forget them.

Later, the same man comments:

> And those discussions in class [in American schools]. They discuss Freud without knowing who Descartes was. Completely idiotic. At least we in our school get the minimum education that is completely necessary and then, after the matriculation *(Bachot),* we are free to continue our education in any way we desire.

Also comparing French and American education, another man says:

> [The French system] is definitely better than the American one, and I can judge because my children go to American schools. The kind of memorizing done in French schools is definitely useful and provides good mental gymnastics, even when it does not result in a great deal of knowledge. It has the advantage of forming the child's mind. A well-formed mind does better, knowledge can be grafted on later *(mieux vaut l'esprit bien formé, les connaissances pourront se greffer ensuite).*

As it is assumed that understanding will follow upon the acquisition of a skill, it is necessary for the child to be given continuous, consistent instruction. Ideally, teaching should be such that mistakes do not occur. Yet it is not expected that learning proceeds without lapses and errors, and even though training is strict, discipline does not exclude a certain interim indulgence. But mistakes are barely tolerated. Good habits should be established as early as possible and mistakes should be continually corrected lest they turn into bad habits.

So, on the one hand, the child is given lengthy practice in repeating the rules, in observing situations, and in carrying out appropriate actions under guidance. And, on the other hand, parents constantly point out how the child should behave and correct errors, emphasizing not so much the need for obedience as the need to learn. Speaking about punishing the child, a man says:

> One tells the child not to do it again (*de ne pas recommencer*). [In punishing the child] one faces it with its responsibility: 'That will teach you to reflect … ' or 'That will teach you to pay attention to what you are doing. 'Above all, it is necessary to point out the good and the bad. It is not like with a dog. The dog, when he does something good, is given a sweet. Recompense, that is stupid. It is necessary that the good should seem good [to the child] and that the bad, in that moment, should seem abnormal …

If the child does not learn well or is flagrantly disobedient, this reflects explicitly on the child, but implicitly on the parents as well, for the good child is one who is *bien élevé* (well brought up) as the bad child is one who is *mal élevé* (badly brought up).[53]

What is done for the child and what the child must do is phrased as necessary for the child's present and, more especially, future well-being. Indeed, an important aspect of teaching is making what is taught *personal* to the one who is learning. Thus, the child is told constantly that it should behave in a certain way for its own sake *(pour soi-même)*. And as part of its formal education, the child is taught how to use models in a "personal" and "original" way. Describing how this is done in French composition lessons in the *lycée*, a woman says:

> For instance, if we were studying in Bruyère, after we had *dictée* and had analyzed passages very carefully and had memorized them, we would be told to go home and write a composition – perhaps a portrait of one of our classmates – in the style of la Bruyère's *Portraits*. We did this with many different kinds of writers …

Or, as another informant explained, the students would be given the outline of an idea in a paragraph, which they would then be expected to expand into an essay in a given style. This gave each student "real scope for originality." In this sense of having assimilated what has been taught, people say that "the French hate conformity … detest uniformity," and so on, and can also assert with confidence, as one young woman did, that

> in our old civilization everyone feels that, no matter how he acts, he acts in a French way …

Implicit in such statements is the belief that individuality consists in the development of new variations on accepted designs. And so, in order to become an individual, the child must learn the design, must make it his own. In this sense, standards are not, in the first instance, personal but exist in the external world and are learned by approximation; once assimilated, they provide the means for and the measure of individual self-expression. Congruent with this is the expectation that the most complex and personally stated idea is communicable if it can be related logically to the traditional and the known. This conception of communicability (which is also related to the idea that the "secret" is knowable but is only selectively known) is important in understanding French attitudes towards the exotic – including both the idea that the exotic is somehow "illogical" and the idea that it may provide new forms of communication[54] – and the attraction and repulsion which the exotic, in different forms at different times, has had for individuals and groups in France.

The ability to make selective use of the traditional in a personal way – or, alternatively, to become an innovator through the use of models other than the traditional ones – is the desired outcome of education. During the earlier stages of learning, the child does not have the capacity for a personal style as it has not yet assimilated the standards on which a personal style is based or in contradistinction to which one may be worked out.

Central to the child's education in the *foyer* and to the formation of the good habits which are regarded as fundamental, is the training given it in connection with food and eating. At table, the learning child is a participant, acted upon and acting, and an audience to adult skill and enjoyment of the delights of the table (*les plaisirs de table)*.

Infants are at first treated essentially as passive receivers of food. Expected to eat as much as they can be made to swallow, the infant and small child are almost literally stuffed with food. Mothers worry lest their infants will not eat enough; loss of appetite is, in fact, a reported childhood "ailment." Transitions from one type of food to another – from milk to the semisolid *bouillies* (at first mainly cereals which may be flavored to make them more palatable even though, it is said, less digestible) and later from *bouillies* to adult foods – are said to be made very gradually as it is important to "habituate" the child to the new foods.[55] The child is not encouraged to feed itself, but is fed by an adult until it is judged able to feed itself "neatly" – at about three years, according to some informants. In learning to eat, as in learning to walk, the young child is protected from capricious behavior – and so from random exploration – by the controlling adults. During this time there is built up, between mother and child, a reciprocal relationship in which the good child responds by eating the food lovingly prepared by the attentive mother.

Children are required to eat everything that is set before them. By the time they eat the same food as adults, they are expected to do so quietly, a silent audience to their parents. *"Mange et tais-toi"* (eat and be quiet) is a commonly remembered admonition. Thus, describing her education, a woman recalled that

> at meals she could never talk but had to eat what was put before her. She only spoke when asking permission to leave the table at the end of meals. She had to eat everything … She could, however, ask her mother very politely if she could have a second helping if there was some food she particularly liked.

And a young man, discussing differences between his adult and childhood enjoyment of food, said:

> I had a very good appetite. Anyway, my father made us willing to eat everything: 'Eat that soup or you won't get anything else.' The next day, at the time when I had my chocolate [in mid-afternoon], I found again the soup which I had refused in the evening. I said to myself: 'It can't go on like that.' I ate the soup. Then I had my chocolate and my piece of bread and butter …

Another woman, commenting on the fact that "children have to eat everything," explained:

> It is much better to force the children to eat everything because otherwise they get too spoiled and grow up to be undisciplined the way Americans do. The Americans misbehaved in France because they lack discipline and you can only have disciplined grown-ups by first disciplining children. [She went on to describe how in her home, when she was a little girl, children had no choice of food, as in America.] But then, in France everything is so delicious.

Agreeing that, although they had no choice, children as well as adults enjoyed eating and later had pleasant memories of good meals, a woman said:

> It's a question of *dressage* (training). People get used to everything. I remember when I was a child the large family meal with uncles and aunts; and they gave even more to *les enfants gourmands* (the greedy children) …

The uncomfortable feeling of being stuffed is associated by adults, recollecting childhood, with the large meals eaten at *fêtes* and family affairs, with the extra tidbits, cakes and *bonbons* given by adults to *"les enfants gourmands."* There is an implied contrast here, between the untrained child who is greedy *(gourmand)* and the trained adult whose taste is selective and controlled (who is a *gourmet)*. Thus, at the same time that the child is obliged to eat every kind of food that is set before it, it is occasionally indulged by being given – at meals where adult conversation is likely to turn on food and also, sometimes, on the effects of over-eating – excessive amounts of particularly delicious food. In this context, both the excellence of the food and the distressing results of having eaten too much are retained in memory.

Adults regard over-eating as an abuse of good food. It is said that adults eat – or should eat – moderately: quality and subtlety of flavoring, especially of sauces, are criteria of delicious food, rather than mere quantity or richness. The meal of many courses is not necessarily a very large one; the separate, perhaps contrasting, courses are arranged to please, not to confuse, the palate. Meals are cooked in terms of an educated palate, trained in appreciation. It is admitted, however, that when cooking is very good, people are likely to eat too much and so, as one woman said, *"abusent de la bonne cuisine francaise,"* with the result that they get *une maladie de foie* and other digestive ailments and then must live at least for a time on a restricted diet. One knows when one has *une maladie de foie* when one has "a feeling of heaviness *(lourdeur)* after a meal and then it is difficult to digest." On the other hand, it is also said to be possible to get *une maladie de foie* from eating poor food – i.e., "bread which isn't bread" (France, 1947), food that is badly prepared, strange and unusual food, foods that are strangely combined, and so on. Asked what circumstances produce *une maladie de foie,* a man replied:

> Living in the colonies. All the people who live in the colonies – and all the English too – have *la maladie de foie.*

Thus, the illnesses categorized as *une maladie de foie* result from *une nourriture pas rationelle* (an irrational diet), or, one might say, from any eating without a rationale.

The experience of feeling stuffed – of being filled either with (too much) good food or with unsuitable food – combined with learning from adult discussions about the effects of *une nourriture pas rationelle,* provides a concrete demonstration of the link between *bonheur* and *malheur,* of the meaning of *bonheur* as a state of balance that is difficult to achieve and likely to be transitory. It seems also that through the experience of childhood stuffing, there is established a concept of a limited internal body space, formulated as follows by Geoffrey Gorer:[56]

> Attention and anxiety are directed on to the proper functioning of the internal organs. Within the limited body space there are a number of

organs whose proper functioning maintains *bonheur,* provided they stay the right size and consistency, but *malheur* is produced if they become swollen (*enflés, gonflés*), or sluggish (*engourdis),* or too heavy *(lourds),* and malfunctioning follows if they become too small (*rétrécis*) or too soft (*mous*). French hypochondriacal fears would seem to be chiefly directed at these eventualities; of these the most common is *la maladie de foie.*

This concept, based on internal and subjective feelings, reflects – as it also is reflected in – a construct of the external world that is limited and compartmentalized both literally and figuratively. Again to quote Gorer's formulation:[57]

> The external world is limited and compartmentalized, both literally and figuratively. The "typical" landscape for Frenchmen is divided into contrasting segments, the greater part of which have been modified by human handiwork. The world of ideas is similarly compartmentalized, and "logic" consists of assigning things and notions to their proper compartments. Correct behavior, which will lead to *bonheur,* demands that the behavior appropriate to a compartment of life be exercised exclusively in that compartment; *malheur* follows inevitably if behavior suitable to one compartment is manifested in another ...

Thus, through food given and received, the child is linked in its first dyadic relationship to another person; through disciplined eating and as an audience to skillful adults the child learns how well-being depends upon an acceptance of limitations and upon the correct channeling of impulse. Family meals also provide the child with a concrete demonstration that pleasure involves reciprocal enjoyment. For not only is food itself a consistent symbol of pleasure,[58] but the cultivation of *les plaisirs de table* is also a shared activity and, as such, provides a model of the essentially social character of pleasure.[59]

Because children are not expected to be able to make reasonable choices, it is up to the parents to decide what is to be done and to set the timing and sequence. Although the mother makes most of the daily decisions, major ones are made by the parents in consultation and may, indeed, involve other adult members of the larger family. The mother selects the clothes bought or made for the children and tells them what to wear on any occasion. The child is considered to have "initiative" when it can follow instructions without daily reminders. And the mother – or both parents – will decide what books the child is to read and at what age it may begin to read them.[60] It is by having selections made for them and by listening to adult conversations about matters of taste that personal taste is formed, slowly and surely.

Learning goes ahead step by step, each one adding a new complication to what is already known. Discussing children's household duties, a woman so describes how she was taught to cook:

> [The mother allowed the girls to cook "nothing at all before fifteen."] At fifteen, or maybe before, we watched her and we could stir the stew or 'put our hands into it, ' as she said, 'to get the feel of it.' At sixteen she began to let us peel the vegetables. She would watch and tease us and tell us it was not good when it was. Then we learned to wash salad. After eighteen and until I married I did half the cooking …

Recognition of the child's development is also a step-by-step matter, involving decisions in which a whole family may express opinions. For instance, a man describes the struggle through which he went before he was permitted to wear long trousers:[61]

> His mother resisted a very long time before she bought him his first pair of long pants and he succeeded in persuading her to do so only after a very long struggle and the intervention of his father on his behalf. Actually, the problem was discussed for days by the entire family. His mother and grandmother argued that he was still a child, while the contrary view was supported by his father, grandfather, and uncle, who maintained that after all when a young man shaved once a week he should be allowed to wear long pants. B. finally won when he was almost sixteen. However, very little change in status and no responsibility came with the acquisition of the coveted long pants …

Parents also are intimately concerned with the child's choice of career. To the extent that the future career is dependent upon decisions made during childhood, these are all made by the parents. Commenting on a fifteen year old American boy who had decided to study physics, a young Frenchman said:

> In France he would have been told: 'You are nothing but a child (*un petit enfant*) – keep still; or better yet, go and amuse yourself in the next room.'

And, speaking about being apprenticed, a lower-middle-class woman said:

> Everyone had to learn a *métier*, boys and girls alike. My father decided that I was to learn dressmaking and my sister typing … I wanted to go on the railroad like my father, but they wouldn't let me. My third sister didn't learn a *métier*. She was the baby and was spoiled by all of us …

Later there is greater freedom of choice: The woman who was a dressmaker's apprentice did in fact become a railroad employée; but looking back on her earlier training she commented, "Look how useful it has been," thus implicitly justifying her parents' decision. And a man, an intellectual with an international background who stressed the freedom of his upbringing, said:

> Our parents left us completely free as to the choice of our careers ...
> When I said my father left us the choice of our careers, it means ... within
> the framework of a liberal university career. Of course, he wouldn't stand
> for our becoming shoemakers or anything of that kind ...

Whether or not the adult carries out the plan laid down by the parents is another question; what is important is that the parents exercise foresight and that the child is generally prepared in terms of some parentally selected *métier* or type of career.

As the child acquires skills in the different spheres of education, it also becomes increasingly able to exercise control. For to be effective, skill must be supported and regulated by control, as it is only by continuous control that the precarious and dignified status of full individuality can be achieved and maintained. Inadequate control or lapses from control bring unpleasant consequences that lead to a decrease in *bonheur* or an increase in *malheur*. As Gorer phrases the point:[62]

> Lack of physical control leads to sickness, above all to diseases of the
> internal organs, and to a lessening of subtle appreciation – *grossièreté*.
> Lack of intellectual control leads to the commission of stupidities – *bêtises*
> ... Lack of emotional control leads to *drames*, over-emotional responses
> which may lead to destruction ... Lack of control of fantasy leads to *les
> désordres des sens*, and so to madness.

By implication, any lack or loss of control carries with it the danger of going to extremes, of becoming, in some sense, a monster (*un monstre*). But it is not the extreme, in and of itself, that is dangerous; it is rather the possibility of going beyond the extreme limit of control into excess and extravagance whether in the direction of denial or indulgence – for both are destructive of humanity, in the French view.

The growing child learns control first through responsive interaction with its parents, its obedience supported by the respect and affection which the child "naturally" feels and by the tenderness and fairness (*justice*) of the parents.

Good habits give it increasing control over its body, including posture and manner of moving. Discussing the relationship of different aspects of control, Jane Belo writes:[63]

> ... the same attitudes which bring about the inhibition of the overt
> expression of aggression in the larger muscles are brought to bear on the
> child to restrain and modify his total posture, the muscular tone of his
> whole body. There are frequent admonitions to *'Tiens-toi bien'* (hold your-
> self well; also, figuratively, behave well). Children are told to sit quietly
> on a bench in the park as part of the exercise of control. Shoulders are not
> rigidly squared as among Germans nor characteristically drooping as
> among some tropical peoples. Hips, like shoulders, seem to move in a

plane, are not rolled or swung. Knees are characteristically held closer together, both by boys and by girls. This rather tense posture learned by the child is carried over by young people, so that the *beau jeune homme,* the *joli garçon* (the handsome young man, the good-looking boy), or the *jeune fille charmante* (the charming young girl) are to be distinguished in posture and gesture from the more settled adults of mature years.[64]

The importance of training in bodily control is reflected especially clearly in the contemporary emphasis in French preschool education upon *l'education sensorielle,* that is, the training of "the eyes, the ears, the touch" and so on, "through exercises such as singing, design, manual work ..." etc. So, for instance, an educator writes:[65]

> The gift of observation is less spontaneous than one would like to say; this so-called gift is acquired by appropriate exercises, exercises which are formal in principle, if you like, because they are contained in an artificially created *ensemble,* but joyously accepted because the exercises are games, true games, animated and passionate.

An important aspect of the teaching of control is immediate adult interference with physically expressed aggression. Fighting among children is not tolerated: children are frequently reminded: "Argue but do not fight" (*Disputez-vous-mais ne vous battez pas*). When children do fight – for instance on the street – it is expected that an adult, even a stranger, will intervene to stop them, and both children are likely to be punished. Among age-mates, the expression of anger and other unsuitable emotions is redirected, is channeled into more acceptable forms of behavior in which the child receives considerable informal and formal training.[66] In the child's relations to its elders, it is required to exercise great control even over verbal expression.

Replying to a comment that there were "no class discussions" in French *lycées,* a woman, herself a teacher, says:

> That is true, but then we in France had great men for our professors; just think, in my time we had in Paris the greatest names – nobody would have dared to contradict them, nobody would even think of doing it ...

And a young man, discussing the same subject, says:

> Actually, I myself was thrown out of a *lycée* after making a disobliging and impolite remark to the professor during a philosophy class. I contradicted him too crudely ...

Qualifying these informants' statements, but congruent with them, is the comment made by another man (an American, educated in French schools) that there was a great deal of exchange between professors and students – at least in advanced classes – but that discussions had to be "of a witty, bantering sort in which the professor himself was not directly attacked." The question is one of skilled control: the student is censured for "crude contradiction."

In another context, describing her difficult, although very affectionate, relationship to her father, a young woman recounts the following incident:

> Several months before my leaving for America we had a terrible quarrel, and then I told my father that I wouldn't discuss any problems with him unless he promised to be calm, to control his emotions, and not to raise his voice. But then, in the middle of the discussion, after he had promised, he began to raise his voice. I became completely mad and began to shout: 'Calm yourself! If you continue to raise your voice I won't go on.' At that moment he grabbed my arm as if he wanted to beat me, but then controlled himself and calmed down. At this moment I realized the enormity of the situation because after all a daughter has no right to calm her father.

Between adults, even parent and child, it becomes exceedingly important for both persons in a potentially explosive situation to maintain control. The child, however, has long since learned when, in its relations to adults, it must remain quiet – as at table it must "eat and keep quiet" and so on. When an older and a younger person have quarreled, it is up to the younger one to apologize; reciprocally, the elder must accept the apology *sans rancune* (without rancour) if the relationship is to be restored.

The child also learns control by being continually occupied in some more or less useful fashion, by not indulging in mere idle daydreams. A young girl says:

> Girls are not allowed to stay idle. No dreaming … they play or knit or do something manual [in their free time]. Listening to the radio for hours is considered bad manners. It is not intelligent … Also reading too many 'silly' novels is bad … C. never saw her mother sitting around doing nothing. Whenever C's mother finds her sitting and thinking, the mother says: *'Allons, allons, assez rêvassé, occupe-toi donc à faire quelque chose.'* (Come, come, enough daydreaming, busy yourself with something.)

It is assumed that, left to their own devices, adolescents will moon about and that measures should be taken lest such dreaming drift too far from possible reality. The heavy school program and the long hours of study required of adolescents are sometimes justified in these terms: the girl or especially the boy is left no time for idle self-indulgence. (It is perhaps significant that, in discussing the problem, French men and women stress not the dreams but rather the countermeasures.)

On the other hand, although learning requires continual effort and application, the performer should give the appearance of ease, of not having made extraordinary efforts. Not the plodder, but the student who appears to have achieved results without special effort is, in the end, admired. A young man says:

> You know, the French don't like to work. This also applies to a great extent to school work. The person who stood first in class was usually the one who was brilliant without having to work too hard at it, while the *bûcheur* (plodder) was usually the one who stood second or third from the top … We like people to think that we succeed *(arrive)* without working too hard for it. Somebody who works too hard to obtain what he wants is an *abruti* (stupified by work). The thing is to appear brilliant and get things through intelligence and brilliance …

Ideally, performance should be so controlled that it shows no signs of the long training involved in mastery. Having learned, the intelligent performer is able to improvise "brilliantly" in response to a new situation.

III. The Foyer: The World Outside

While the child is learning, it lives within a restrictive, protecting *milieu*, the dimensions of which only gradually expand. As the space widens within which the child moves safely, direct adult supervision of its activities is also gradually reduced. Yet the circle of the *foyer* with its established relationships, in which everyone is believed to be entirely secure as long as there is no intruding interference, is and remains central to the child's life.

Just as the infant was "menaced" by various external dangers from which it was protected by its parents' care, so the child too is felt to be threatened by various dangers – sometimes precisely, sometimes only vaguely perceived and formulated – in the open environment beyond the *foyer*.

Recalling his childhood, Pierre Loti describes the impact of such dangers on the child's imagination:

> My mother had departed, and it gave my heart a feeling of heaviness to know that she was out. Out in the streets! I was content not to be there where it was cold and dark, there where little children so easily lost their way, – how snug it was to be within doors before the fire that warmed me through and through; how nice it was to be at home! … I was sadly troubled at the thought of the immense, strange world lying beyond the door.

And further:

> What I feared to see enter that door [to the dark hall] had no well defined form, but the fear was none the less definite to me: and it kept me standing motionless near the dead fire with wide-open eyes and fluttering heart. When my mother suddenly entered the room by a different door, oh! how I clung to her and covered my face with her dress: it was a supreme protection, the sanctuary where no harm could reach me, the harbor of harbors where the storm is forgotten ….

For the child, the dangers beyond the *foyer* may be personified in the bogey figures about which the child is told and with which it may be threatened. Speaking of children going out alone, a husband and a wife explain:

> *Husband:* In my part of the country, it is quite regular, children are warned that if they go about alone the *loup-garou* or *ramponneau* will get them …
>
> *Wife* [somewhat later in the conversation]: … in Paris they didn't say anything like that, but in the country we were told that the *gendarmes* would get us. (Husband concurs.) And we were also frightened of *gens*

> *contrefaits* (deformed people) and village idiots … [in Paris] mother
> impressed on me that if anybody spoke to me in the streets I was not to
> reply and not to follow them. When I was a child there was the notorious
> Soleilland case and it had much impressed mother and frightened her …

From one point of view, then, the world beyond the *foyer* is inhabited
by people who represent threats to the safety of the inexperienced
child (i. e., persons who are strange, whose appearance and behavior
are perhaps unusual and seem inexplicable, suggesting the idea of the
sadistic murderers or the childhood bogeys).[68]

From another point of view, this external world presents oppor-
tunities that are dangerous to the child who is exposed to them pre-
maturely, without guidance and supervision. So, a father (who has
just told his eighteen and twenty year old sons to come home before
midnight) says that

> he always likes to know where his children are and what they are doing,
> because "what can a young boy be doing after twelve o'clock but some-
> thing he shouldn't be doing?"

By implication, it is the child's inadequacy – its still incomplete
knowledge, the uncertainty of its skill and control, the assumption
that it may act upon "caprice" – that makes the unforeseen situation,
the unexpected opportunity, dangerous: "If one leaves the child to
himself, one will be making a misfit." Not experimentation with the
unknown, but experience gained in a safe context under the guidance
of those who have already learned, gives the poise and assurance necessary to adult competence.

Without initiation and without guidance, even relationships
with a deep and permanent value, representing the individual's most
personal choices – love and friendship – may become a danger to
himself and others. Thus, in French fiction, a contrasting theme to
that of the older man who gives way to impulses that are no longer
suitable, is that of the boy or young man (and the girl) who becomes
involved in situations, relationships, and responsibilities proper to
the adult.[69]

From these various dangers, however presented and perceived,
the child is protected by the restrictions placed upon its activities. The
young child is not permitted to go out unaccompanied; the older
child must account strictly for time spent away from home. Outside
of the immediate family, the child's first companions are likely to be
cousins, its first friends chosen from among schoolmates. Speaking of
her relations to others of her own age, a young woman says:

The children I used to see most of were my cousins of both sexes. That was until the age of twelve. After that, I joined the scouts and made some friends there. But still I continued to see my immediate family …

… And my parents always knew my friends; it is unavoidable because they all belonged to more or less the same social circle and if at first they didn't know each other, they knew about each other and would finally meet on a special occasion. It was probably while taking their children to their [the children's school friends'] parties. My parents wouldn't let me go visit people whom they didn't know …

… I started to go out alone, but only to school, at the age of thirteen. Also I would be allowed to go out sometimes in the company of other girls …

Yet, for the growing child, the ties formed with its age-mates become increasingly important as a source of enjoyment and a focus of interest. Initially, a safe area – outside the *foyer* but safe for the child – within which friendships can be formed is provided by the parents and parent surrogates. Not only is the area closely guarded, but the children themselves are constrained in various ways by the parents and others responsible for them. For the city child, the small, often enclosed park with its benches and gravelled paths and formal lawns and ornamental shrubbery is a place where it can meet and play with other children within sight and reach of guardian adults.[70] Here the parent's role appears to be mainly a protective and restraining one. Parents (or nurses) watch over their own children – feed them, talk to them, correct them, sometimes initiate and facilitate play – but seem to show little interest in other nearby groups of adults and children, unless their own charges have been interfered with or seem to be interfering. When children play together, it is more or less on their own initiative. In her description of children's play in two parks in Paris, Martha Wolfenstein comments:[71]

Positive attitudes and behavior of children towards each other seemed to get no adult approval, reinforcement or urging, whether between children in the same family or playmates. The attitude of the adults here seemed very different from that of American mothers who are so anxious for their children to make friends, encouraging older children in the family to play with younger ones, etc. The children I observed showed many positive feelings towards each other, which went apparently unnoticed by adults and seemed to constitute an almost clandestine bond between the children. Adult interference with children's behavior towards each other seemed to be confined to cases of negative behavior …

And again:[71]

Mothers seemed inclined to suppose that their children's approaches to other children were more negatively motivated than was the case.

The children were observed to approach one another with interest and sympathy, even though their friendliness was not given positive support by the accompanying adults. Children's intimacy exists, as it were, apart from the adults. So, for instance, two brothers (five and six years old) are described as they take a walk suggested to them by their father:[71]

> As they get farther away from the father, the boys begin putting their arms around each other's shoulders. They become more animated and point things out to each other as they go along. As they get nearer to the father again on the return path, they drop their arms from each other's shoulders, drift apart, and again become subdued.

Small play groups of children also showed a definite *esprit de corps* with reference to those included and excluded, as is illustrated in the following incident:[71]

> There was a definite feminine *esprit de corps* about the girls' group work-ing on the 'garden' [made of pebbles on a path]. While boys were excluded, girls were welcomed into the group. A quiet four year old girl enters the 'garden' and is gradually assimilated from bystander to partic-ipant. The seven year old leader bends down and embraces her, asks her to *'nous aider,'* to work like a *'nègre, '* as they start laying out more rows of pebbles. Later the feminine monopoly of the garden is made explicit when the six year old pushes out another five year old boy and says: 'Boys aren't allowed in the garden, only girls.' ... There was also a con-tinuous exclusion of younger children from the play of the girls. When these children wander into the 'garden' they are told in a mildly exasper-ated tone that they spoil the *allées*. Children of two or under are picked up gently under the arms and carried over the boundaries ... The adults sitting by do not ask the older children to include the younger ones.

In the parks the parents provide an appropriate place for chil-dren to play. They keep the children there safely and prevent them from acting in hostile ways to other children, but leave the forma-tion of friendly relations more or less within the control of the chil-dren themselves.

Similarly, when the child goes to school, personal discipline is enforced mainly to prevent disturbing outbursts, but little is done to foster friendly relationships among the children. By this time chil-dren are expected to have learned ways of handling anger, jealousy, and so on; they themselves are said to deplore and control actual fighting. An American man, for instance, recalls how his French class-mates in a Parisian *lycée* reacted to a fistfight between himself and a Russian boy with "an icy silence that lasted for several days." Adults limit their interference to situations that appear to be getting out of hand: they will intervene, on the one hand, when quarrels threaten to turn violent; or, on the other hand, when, between friends, there is too open expression of intense intimacy. Within these limits upon the expression of feeling, the first possibly lasting friendships are formed with persons not connected with the *foyer.*

In contrast to the relationships of members of the *foyer* and the larger family to one another, school friendships – like the friendships formed by adults – are based upon mutual choice, upon the recognition of a common interest and special congeniality *(sympathie)*. Such school friendships are placed in a particular category by adults. For instance, school friends may continue to address each other as *tu* (second person singular, in intimate and familiar address), even though as time goes on the pair may no longer be intimate.[72] This is characteristic of few friendships formed in later years. School friendships may be exceedingly intense, or they may be merely comradely – individual relationships within a larger clique. Friendships, like relationships within the *foyer,* also tend to be dyadic – exclusive relationships between a pair of individuals. It is the element of *choice* that differentiates friendship from a familial relationship: whereas within the *foyer* mutuality is based upon "natural" and "instinctive" emotions, between friends affection and loyalty affirm each partner's selection of the other.

School friendships may exist quite apart from the *foyers* of either or both children. For even though children may be permitted to visit only those friends whose parents are known and approved, this does not preclude friendships with other children: it merely sets limits upon the time and circumstances of their meetings. This in itself emphasizes the privacy of friendship. Furthermore, as friendships are personally defined, each child in a *foyer* may form its own circle of companions with each of whom it may share experiences in which no outsider – not even a trusted brother or sister – participates.

Throughout the school years, friendships are formed along sex lines: boys with boys, girls with girls. This reflects and sets a pattern that is maintained throughout life as far as friendship is concerned. For, in the French view, this relationship is, almost by definition, one between two men or two women, in which sexual aspects are sublimated or excluded. In these special terms it may be said – more readily by men than by women – that heterosexual friendships are not possible; not inconsistently, people speak of "exceptional" cases where the sexual possibilities of a relationship between a man and a woman have not been realized or where the basis of the relationship has altered over a period of time. In this connection, it is significant that the meaning of *ami* changes radically as it is used by a speaker in reference to someone of his own or opposite sex. When a man speaks of *mon ami* (referring to a man), he is talking about a friend; when he speaks of his *petite amie,* he means his mistress, usually a girl of a social class lower than his own.[73] An exception to this is the *amitié amoureuse,* in which the link between love and friendship in a relationship between a man and a woman is given open recognition; what is recognized, however, is essentially intensity of feeling, for the relationship is definitely one that is not overtly sexual and yet, as the phrase *amitié amoureuse* implies, has warmer emotional undertones than friendship, as such. For relationships less personal than friendship, slang expressions such as *copain* and *copine* (pal) are sometimes used (heterosexual relationships are included here), particularly to refer to comradeship among rather young people or among men and women working together in a group.

Whether or not they are lasting, school friendships represent one of the first important ways in which individuality can be expressed and affirmed through wholly personal choice. School friendships tend to drop into the background – especially among men – as other more diversified interests take precedence; in their main characteristics, however, they prefigure one type of deeply valued adult relationship in which the self is defined, in part, through an interest shared with another person of the same sex.

Friendship is, of course, only one of several different kinds of relationship that are entered into during the years when the boy and girl are living in their parental home and that shape the adult's view of the world in which he moves. For instance, during their student years men[74] may enter into dyadic rivalries that are as enduring as friendships; these are at least indirectly fostered – in professional circles – by the examination and formal career systems. However, friendship – especially between men – is the relationship outside the *foyer* that is consistently and sharply defined, and that is regarded as valuable to the adolescent as to the adult.

The young boy or girl is, however, considered incompetent to make meaningful heterosexual choices. The boy must first learn from older, more experienced women how to manage his sexual life. Thus, he learns outside the *foyer* (with the help or condonation of his father) and in relationships that are transitory and more or less clandestine, skills that will be important in his own *foyer*. The girl, on the contrary, though she is taught how to be feminine within the protection of the parental *foyer,* is kept inexperienced until she marries. In this traditional ordering of life, heterosexuality is continuously viewed in adult terms, in which the initial matching of experience and inexperience is only one expression of expected contrast between the man and the woman. Two women – mother and daughter, elder and younger sister, friend and friend (where a friendship breaks down) – may become rivals for a man; two men – father and son – may become rivals for a younger woman. But both friendship and love, the two most important relationships of choice, are regarded as essentially nonrivalrous and noncompetitive: friendship because it is based on mutual likeness, love because it is based upon matching contrast. By compartmentalizing these two types of relationship – by emphasizing the contrast between them – adult relationships within and without the *foyer* involve personal choice but are given a quite different basis for stability.

In adult life, one extension of the dyadic relationship of friends is that of the small, sometimes quite heterogeneous group drawn together through the relationship each has to one individual: then the common friendship may have the effect of fostering a linked series of friendships among all the others. The group of students around an admired teacher and the literary salon are traditional examples of such small linked circles. The central person in such a group (who is, in effect, the hub of the wheel) may or may not be someone with formal prestige; it is more important that he (or she) combine the ability to act simultaneously in a variety of personal relationships with special skill in interpreting one individual to another. It is characteristic of such groups that they are held together by a common interest or a common experience which provides a point of contact for people who may share little else. So, for instance, a woman informant, herself a key figure in several small circles, described a number of these groups including, during World War II, cliques formed in Paris markets by women who bought from a certain vendor and who protected one another's interests and the "families" formed by French civil prisoners in German jails and concentration camps. In some of these "families" the strong sense of identity and mutual responsibility far outlasted the dispersal of the members during and after the war. In such situations, the common bond of interest so essential to friendship was provided by shared circumstance rather than idea or belief.[75]

Ideally, complete individuality depends upon – as it develops out of – a person's capacity to belong to a variety of diverse groups, keeping the interests of each separate – even though his place in one may be enhanced by his reputation made in another – and maintaining his sense of being himself in all of them. For it is not the specialist, as such, who is most admired in France but rather the man who can balance two separate careers, who can make himself felt in *milieux* where his particular talents and skills are of no specific importance, the cultivated man who can respond brilliantly to a variety of persons in different contexts. From one point of view, indeed, it can be said that French individualism consists precisely in this capacity to share common interests selectively in a variety of relationships involving choice and a limited but very personal commitment to each.

For the French, the stranger *(l'étranger)* is essentially the outsider, not necessarily someone who is unknown *(inconnu)*, but rather the identified alien with whom one has no common bonds and about whose intentions there is no certainty. Thus, a young woman says:

> *L'étranger?* You have to distinguish between *le sens propre* and *le sens figuré* (the literal and the figurative meanings). When you come to a village you are *inconnu* (unknown). But if you come and identify yourself, you are *l'étranger* ... Camus' title [L'Etranger] is in the *sens figuré* – someone not like the others ...

So *l'étranger* refers to the person who is "alien" in the widest as well as in the narrowest meaning of this word. He may be someone from another neighborhood or town or region of France, or he may be a foreigner – an Italian who has lived and worked for twenty years in Provence, and so on. He is someone "not like the others ..." and, living where he does not belong, he is *déraciné* – without roots. The stranger is, in fact, anyone who belongs outside the safe confines of the *foyer*. There its members may establish relationships with him, providing these do not disturb or conflict with the interests of the *foyer*. Who is regarded as a stranger depends upon the context. The idea of the *foyer* may be extended to the circles to which the individual belongs, or it may include all of France (as when, for instance, newspaper writers refer to *le foyer national)*; in some circumstances, the whole of the French empire may be included (when, from one point of view, a native people may be regarded as *les étrangers* in the process of assimilation);[76] in other circumstances (as when, making some comparison, a Frenchman says in self-reference, "we Europeans"), western Europe may be the *foyer* to be defended from encroachment from East and West.

Attitudes towards the stranger in one's midst are markedly ambivalent. On the one hand, there are recognized roles for strangers within France (as there are also clearly recognized deviant roles for the French) and the person who is identified as filling one of these, although not necessarily liked, is tolerated and may be highly esteemed. For accepted strangers include not only those who are recognized as making some contribution to French civilization, and those who are friends – men and women who stand in an intermediary position between the French and their own compatriots – but also, in varying degrees groups who are pejoratively described as *les sales étrangers* (dirty strangers), etc. As long as strangers continue to act in ways that are expected of them – however un-French – they are safely familiar.

At the same time, there is underlying anxiety about the stranger based on a sense of the uncertainty of communication and on associations of the strange with the potentially dangerous. The outsider is viewed as a potential intruder and creator of confusion and disturbance; not knowing what the limits are, he may have to be restrained forcibly in self-defense. With the outsider who is identified as amicable, there is nevertheless the danger of a break in communications; when he is identified as a possible enemy, there is the additional danger of intentional hostile intrusion. The stranger who learns to appreciate French values and who strikes roots in France becomes more comprehensible and comprehending, yet he may also be the more dangerous for, in contrast both to the friend (and an outsider can be formally made *un ami de France)* who retains his identity and his previous loyalties and to *l'ennemi déclaré* (the enemy who openly defines his position),[77] the apparently assimilated stranger may destroy from within because he is not recognizable.[78] He, especially, may be *le monstre* – in fantasy combining the dehumanized features of the bogey and the "unnatural" person.[79]

There is, when the outsider is included within the picture, an essential conflict between the belief that as French values can be articulately expressed, they can be taught and learned (and consequently in varying degrees are available to outsiders whether in France or abroad) and the belief that only those born and reared in a French *foyer* in France can be completely French and can fully understand and be understood by other Frenchmen. Like the adopted child which – though it becomes part of a *foyer,* is irrevocably changed by its familial training, and contributes to *le bonheur du foyer* – only doubtfully belongs to its adoptive family, the Frenchman going abroad may acquire a new citizenship without – in French eyes – ceasing to be French, and the stranger in France, no matter how well he has learned all that can be explicitly taught, remains "a little different from the others." The conflict can be resolved at two levels, i.e., in the belief that French values are also universal values, and in the expectation that while personal relationships require a meeting point in terms of which both partners can respond, they involve a segment rather than the whole of experience. But, in fact, since the maintenance of adulthood and the achievement of *bonheur* depend upon training in skills and control that is begun in the *foyer,* long before formal education begins, the conflict remains and the stranger is both attractive (as he may suggest new models) and threatening (as he may intrude and destroy what he does not understand).

But for the Frenchman at home among other French people these beliefs are mutually supporting as they ensure the security of the individual and the stability of the society. Upbringing within the *foyer,* the conscious use of models which must be assimilated before the learner ceases to be an apprentice, the expectation that, having acquired skill and control, the adult can improvise and the improvisations will be understood – all this ensures communication among those who, having this training in common, define themselves primarily as "individualists." This is expressed by a contemporary French writer as he attempts to define the universal meaning of civilization:[80]

> A civilization is a common way of living, of feeling and of thinking, a scale of values and a style; it draws into relief *(relève)* certain organizing principles which are more or less explicit, yet which inform (*informant* – i.e. are implicit in) the beliefs, the institutions, and the artifacts (*les oeuvres)* and, through their interpretation, imprint themselves *(s'imposent)* on intellects and hearts; thus they are transmitted from generation to generation.

Implicit in this statement is a conception of stability in which the past is continually incorporated into the present and provides models for the future; in which the individual is formed by his civilization, exemplifies it and, in so doing, creatively renews rather than alters it. This is, in fact, but another way of stating the aims of French education *(formation).*

NOTES

1. This presentation is based upon the work of all those in Research in Contemporary Cultures, mainly members of the French group, who contributed to the study of French culture, modified by my own understanding of the subject. I am indebted especially to those upon whose interviews with French informants and previously formulated insights I have drawn very extensively, with and without specific acknowledgment, i.e., Theodora M. Abel, Jane Belo, Nicholas Calas, Helen Garrett, Geoffrey Gorer (who was the first convener of the French group and who framed a set of tentative working hypotheses on which much of the subsequent research by the group was based), Nelly S. Hoyt, Paulette Leshan, Nathan Leites, Margaret Mead, Irene Rozeney, Allan Ullman, and Martha Wolfenstein. This discussion of the *foyer* encompasses only part of the work done by the group though it draws upon the work as a whole; the responsibility for its organization and the presentation of ideas therein devolves upon myself.

2. All quotations from statements by French men and women and by other persons on France are taken from interviews with informants conducted by members of the French group in Research in Contemporary Cultures. Except where, occasionally, the translation of a French term has been inserted, the quotations are given here as recorded by the original interviewers. The interviews are contained in the files of manuscripts on French culture now in the custodianship of the Institute for Intercultural Studies, New York.

3. The image of the *foyer* is, however, also used in a much more generalized way by French writers. Thus, in connection with French colonialism, an historian comments: "La France a toujours cherché à se répandre au dehors ... Son naturel sociable tend à élargir sans cesse le cercle de la famille et à multiplier les foyers." (Gabriel Hanotaux: *Histoire des Colonies Françaises,* Vol. I, *Introduction Générale,* p. 1. Paris: Plon, 1929.)

4. Translated excerpt from a letter written to the newspaper, *France-Amerique,* in a contest for French war brides, December, 1946.

5. See especially L. C. Jouanneau (editor): *Discussions du Code Civil dans le Conseil d'Etat,* 3 volumes (Paris, 1805-8), and *Travaux de la Commission de Réforme du Code Civilt Année 1945-1946* (Paris: Recueil Sirey, 1947).

6. Jouanneau, *op cit.* Vol. 1, pp. 448, 449. The speaker is Trenchet, a conservative member of the Conseil d'Etat. Translated.

7. The prospective parents of an adopted child must have been married a specific length of time and have reached a certain age before they may qualify as adopters. Further legal reforms, now under consideration, would reduce the *minimum* requirements of age and length of time married; thus, protection of the as yet unborn natural child is still regarded as central to the problem.

8. Under certain circumstances, a child who is adopted or who has lived in the adopting family before the age of five, may have all reference to its actual origin removed from its birth certificate and other legal docu-

ments. Thus, by a legal fiction, the child is made a full member of the adopting family. By this means stigma is removed from the child who is adopted (for then "nobody need know") – but not from *adoption*. At the same time, institutions informally discourage the adoption of infants (foundlings and abandoned children) who are less than eighteen months of age because "the child's first claim is on its own mother" and "the family may yet be brought together ... especially if it is the first child." In such situations also, the emphasis is upon maintaining or creating a true *foyer*. It is significant that although the number of adoptions given legal protection has enormously increased in the past fifty years (from about 50 in 1900 to more than 2,000 in 1944), the absolute number is not very large even today. For a detailed discussion, cf. Marcel Vismard: *Traité théorique et pratique de l'adoption et de la légitimation adoptive* (Paris: Recueil Sirey, 1951).

9.   *Adoption* (pamphlet) (Montevrain (S. -et-M.): Imprimerie de l'Ecole d'Alembert, 1948), p. 1. Translated.

10. Geoffrey Gorer: "French Culture – Preliminary Hypotheses."

11. The French handling of this theme is discussed in some detail by Martha Wolfenstein and Nathan Leites in *Movies: A Psychological Study* (Glencoe, Illinois: Free Press, 1950).

12. However, there are in France various kinds of ritualized fighting associated with special groups or special circumstances. Thus, dueling was traditionally aristocratic; street fighting at certain times is considered part of student life; boxing (until recently) was regarded mainly as a proletarian preoccupation. A generation ago, Parisian school boys might be taught two very formal types of fighting as a sport, i.e., *savate* and a special kind of fencing with a cane. (For illustrations of both of these, cf. *Petit Larousse Illustré;* Paris: Librairie Larousse, 1908, pp. 125 and 147.) Speaking of *les exercises de canne,* an informant recalled that his instructor had told the school boys that this was a most useful and necessary defense against rowdies and "tough guys" who might attack young men at night on the streets.

   Again, in connection with bull fighting in southern France, although there are many French enthusiasts, there is a general belief that the actual participants are all foreigners. That is, the enthusiasm of the spectator is safeguarded by defining the performer – whose skills are admired – as someone who is different (i.e., the performer is a foreigner, an outsider).

13. An excellent phrasing of the French attitude toward reciprocity is given by Claude Lévi-Strauss in his chapter, "Le Principe de Réciprocité," in *Les Structures élémentaires de la parenté* (Paris: Presses Universitaires de France, 1949), especially pp. 74-76, where he describes the relationship between strangers in a restaurant, seated at one table and exchanging the wine served with their meal, then, as he puts it, "... the wine given invokes the wine returned, cordiality requires cordiality ... And acceptance of the offer authorizes another offer, that of conversation" (p. 76).

14. This is, of course, an illustration of one aspect of dyadic relationships already discussed. The theme is treated in many variations in novels so

that only a few examples need be cited here: Balzac: *La Cousine Bette* and *Mémoires de deux jeunes mariées;* Daudet: *Froment jeune et Risler aîné;* Duhamel: *Chronique* des *Pasquier;* Martin du Gard: *Les Thibault;* Romain: *Les hommes de bonne volonté* (e. g., the incidents involving the family of Louis Bastide); Gide: *L'école des femmes* and *Robert;* and so on.

15. The highly ambivalent attitude toward the *fille mère* (unmarried mother) and her child and toward the orphans and abandoned children cared for by the *Assistance Publique,* illustrate this point. The relative emphasis upon the family with children in contemporary French social legislation, is another illustration. For it is not merely adults as such, but rather those adults who have or who may be expected to have children who are the major beneficiaries of the new social laws; by comparison, as one man commented, "the single person has a harder time than ever."

16. So, on the one hand, there is the belief that – if not nowadays, then formerly – orphan girls, brought up by the *Assistance Publique,* were sexually victimized when they became servants in peasant households: "… These girls are cattle for sleeping with *(bétail qui couche)* and if they refuse they may be beaten and even smothered …" a man said, describing a situation he knew by hearsay. Or, on the other hand, there is the belief that the hated *Gardes Mobiles* were recruited from among boys educated by the *Assistance Publique;* an alternative, but not incongruent, belief is that these police are Corsicans, that is, that they are essentially foreigners.

17. For the handling of such figures in French movies, one may cite such films as *Panique* – in which the central character is an elderly man who has been deserted by his wife, a stranger who is finally driven to death by an uncomprehending mob; *Le Corbeau,* in which the central theme is the danger to the community of unauthorized private information revealed in poison-pen letters, and in which the main characters are a childless couple; a widower who has lost his wife in childbirth and who has tried to conceal his identity; a young woman on the verge of becoming an old maid; an embittered old maid who has lost her fiancé to another woman; a widow whose war-hero son is driven to suicide; etc.

18. A whole series of films made in France during the past twenty years have had as one theme the reconstitution of the *foyer,* in the development of which a child is a crucial figure, though not always central to the plot. Among others, one may cite *La Maternelle, La Fille du Puisatier, Harvest,* and the *Marius – Fanny-César* trilogy. In the last, a child is first given a respectable *foyer* when an elderly widower marries a girl who has been deserted by her young lover; later, when the "father" dies, the child is instrumental in reuniting the true parents. The recent film, *Passion for Life,* which is intended to be a plea for educational reform, is emotionally built around the regeneration of a war orphan through his acquisition of a father (his understanding teacher from whom he learns about the "rights of man," i. e., learns to be human), a mother (another teacher – who replaces an inadequate sister), and, in fact, a complete set of relatives as the entire village participates in his final struggle to be accepted as a normal person (symbolized by his taking and passing his school examinations).

The theme of the child becoming a fully human individual through participation in a *foyer* is stated in reverse in a recent novel, *Les Jeux Inconnus* by François Boyer (Paris: Les éditions de minuit, 1947). Here a child, whose parents are killed during the mad rush of refugees from cities during the fall of France and who is rejected by distracted parents separated from their own children, is no longer able to distinguish between reality and fantasy, between human and animal; deprived of meaningful relationships, the child herself becomes an unwitting destroyer, bringing about the death of the one person – another child – who treats her humanly.

It is not without significance that a child (in *Passion for Life* and *Les Jeux Inconnus,* for instance) is selected as a symbol of a world in change – in which alternative solutions are offered: on the one hand, reintegration into normal life through the intervention of insightful adult parent figures; on the other hand, destruction through the hands of an unguided and disoriented child. In another – and apparently highly disturbing – film made in the 1930's, *Zero for Conduct,* a futile children's rebellion in a school appears to symbolize the *impasse* of a world in which communication between two generations has broken down. Presented (by adults) as a child's view of the adult world, this film confirms, by denial, the meaning of the *foyer.*

19. It is regarded as a desirable thing when working wife and husband complement each other in their skills. Thus, it is not unusual for teachers in a rural school to be husband and wife – one teaching the elder, the other the younger children; or one teaching the boys, the other the girls. Or husband and wife may have a joint business enterprise (i. e., a restaurant or cafe) in which their responsibilities are complementary. There is a belief that such working couples are childless, the business to some extent supplanting the *foyer* in their interests. If there are children, it is not unusual for them to be sent away from home (to grandparents, to farm-homes, or to schools) to board. This willingness on the part of French men and women to accept the idea of women working away from home (which does not mean having "outside interests") and the expectation that children may then have to be brought up elsewhere are both part of the total picture but do not, it would seem, invalidate the ideal of the *foyer.*

20. This phrase, *faire quelque chose de rien,* is also used to describe the cleverness with which a woman has made herself a dress (*une petite robe)* or a hat, "out of nothing."

21. Interview by Tex McCrary and Jinx Falkenburg. "New York Close-Up" *New York Herald Tribune,* November 23, 1951).

22. In contemporary France there is some evidence of a changing attitude toward marital infidelity, which is explained in terms of material circumstances – "Nowadays a man would certainly be depriving his family of necessary money if he had a mistress"; or, "Only war profiteers can afford to have mistresses ..." (both statements by men). The relationship of this change of attitude to the greater freedom of the young girl and the employed woman is a problem for future exploration.

23. It is significant that strangers and eccentric characters, as portrayed in fiction (sometimes individuals without a known *foyer* – see above Notes 16 and 17), may in appearance and/or character suggest qualities associated with the childhood bogey. Characteristics of the bogey can also be seen in cartoons, e. g., those in which the enemy is depicted as a heavy, crushing boot. Nonhuman bogey figures also appear in the responses of our informants to the Rorschach inkblot test. On the Rorschach blots our subjects responded with remarkable regularity to re-evocation of monsters, usually mythological and creatures of the night, vague, dark and threatening. Card IV (regarded by some Rorschach workers as particularly evocative of the father image) elicited the largest number of direct references to a menacing dark monster. One woman informant called Card IV *"un monstre"* (a monster). She then elaborated in the inquiry by saying ..., "Have you heard the story of the tree that moved and which is a monster, enormous, terrible, ready to attack someone, heavy and horrible, walking ponderously ?" ... Repeatedly this night-time figure occurred among our subjects, not only on Card IV, but also on Cards I, V, and VI as well, mostly characterized as a monster, or bird of prey and death, but sometimes in other terms, once as the *croque-mitaine* himself, another time as a German or Russian with heavy boot (Card IV). The war orphan French children also saw ogres, serpents, and big men on the achromatic Rorschach blots. (Cf. Abel, Belo, and Wolfenstein: "An Analysis of French Projective Tests," in Part II of this volume, pp. 140-60.)

24. Women's statements on this point reflect their own beliefs rather than the factual situation; men's statements are conflicting. Further investigation is needed here.

25. See, for instance, Gide's description of his early relationship to his father, and his memory of his father addressing him as his "little friend." The father is, however, pictured as busy and secluded in his study, where the little boy goes only by invitation. (If It Die ... Translated by Dorothy Bussy. London: Seeker and Warburg, 1951, pp. 8ff.)

26. Cf. Wolfenstein and Leites: *Movies, op. cit., passim,* for a detailed analysis of this theme in contemporary French films. In this presentation I have also drawn upon an unpublished discussion of the subject by Jane Belo: "The Father Image."

27. Wolfenstein and Leites, *Movies,* p. 163.

28. See above, pp. 33 -34 – informants' use of the image of "the king" in comparing the relative positions of husband and wife in France and the United States.

29. It is not possible to say to what extent the problem of how the sexual enlightenment of the young girl is to be handled is accentuated by being moved from a French to an American environment, where dating patterns are dependent upon the girl's ability to take care of herself. This is in sharp contrast to the traditional French situation, where the *jeune fille,* regarded as "something very precious," is protected by a wall of reserve placed around her and by restrictions on her activities. However, as the kind and amount of protection given the *jeune fille* in France is altering

very rapidly, it is quite likely that mother and daughter find themselves in a quandary in France as well as when they come to the United States.

30. In recent years there has been a significant change in the general availability of medical care and advice in connection with public services provided for maternal and infant welfare. Information is lacking about ways in which women are taking advantage of this new situation and about the effects of such professionally given advice and assistance (which are directed primarily to the young woman with a new family) upon the relationship of mother and adult daughter. Although acceptance of such advice would seem to be congruent with other modifications of the mother-daughter relationship that appear to be taking place (i. e., a lessening of the adult daughter's dependence upon her mother), it would be important to know whether, for instance, professional advice about child care becomes an alternative to or is phrased as a form of "maternal advice" and how it may be modified in practice in terms of the mother's own experience imparted to the young married daughter, etc.

31. The French film, *Grand Illusion,* in which the pacifist theme is supported by the implicit theme of the relationship of an elder and two younger brothers in a hostile world, is one illustration of the depth of meaning of *fraternité* for the French.

32. See Wolfenstein and Leites, *Movies, passim,* for an analysis of this theme. The recent romantic comedy, *Marie du Port,* combines in one film the theme of father-son rivalry for a young woman and that of sister rivalry for one man. In this particular case a happy solution is worked out for all four, in which the younger sister marries the elder sister's former lover, while the elder sister takes over and educates the younger sister's rejected suitor.

33. Data are lacking on the details of adult brother-sister relationships and of other relationships between men and women based on the same model, though data are sufficient to indicate that this would prove a rewarding area of investigation.

34. The dramatic handling of this conception by the French is discussed by Martha Wolfenstein and Nathan Leites in "An Analysis of French Films," (see below, Part II, pp. 100-139). There they conclude (p. 138):

> French films may be compared with two contrasting types of drama. In one, we see the just triumph of the hero, based on the denial and projection of forbidden wishes. This is the major pattern of American films. In the other, we see the just death of the hero, following from the explicit or implicit acknowledgment of forbidden wishes, the pattern of classical and Shakespearean tragedy. Both of these dramatic types, while differing from each other, revolve around moral issues. In contrast to both, French films emphasize the acknowledgment of reality rather than fantasy of a moral order. They show repeatedly that deprivations and rewards may be equally undeserved. The events of real life do not coincide with justice. There is no supernatural justice, and human authorities are incompetent either to find out the facts or to understand men's souls. Nor is the world arranged to satisfy human wishes. Something happening a moment sooner or

a moment later may make all the difference between our happiness and ruin; but this is mere chance. The reiteration of these not easily acceptable facts may help us to reduce disappointment by not expecting, too much. A little, fragile, brief pleasure is possible in life, though by no means assured; but we will only jeopardize it if we demand the impossible. Underneath this acceptance of disappointment, and facilitating it, there may be … unadmitted feelings of guilt. However, they do not give rise to the tragedy of moral punishment. Life in its very nature punishes us sufficiently.

35. Translated from *Petit Guide de la jeune maman avant et apès la naissance* (Editions Sociales Françaises, n.d.), p. 53. One meaning of *paresseux* is "dunce." This statement may be compared to an equivalent American one, also in a child care manual: "Most babies take to the breast very well … When he feels the nipple near his mouth he will 'root around' trying to get hold of it … Daring the first week it may be better to stop him after fifteen minutes …" etc. (Benjamin Spock: *The Pocket Book of Baby and Child Care.* New York: Pocket Books, 1946, p. 34.) In our American conception, it is the mother, not the infant, who may be unready and unsure.

36. Translated from P. Lereboullet and others: *Le Guide de la jeune mère,* 8th edition (Paris: Les Editions Sociales Françaises, 1947), p. 50.

37. Translated from P. Lereboullet: *Manuel de Puériculture,* 5th edition rev. (Paris: Masson, 1949), p. 4. Note that in this sentence *"progressivement"* conveys the idea of slow gradualness, which contrasts sharply to the American meaning of "progress."

38. Ibid., p. 123.

39. Ibid., p. 154.

40. Jouanneau; *Discussions du Code Civil dans le Conseil d'Etat,* Vol. 1, p. 490.

41. Cf. *Travaux de la Commission* de *Réforme du Code Civil.*

42. It appears that, as regards discipline, child care manuals, written by professional people, echo men's answers to women's complaints about children's disobedience, e.g., "You (the mother) should be more strict with them." They are in contrast to adult recollections of the mother as strict but close to the children. It is as if in their discussions of disciplinary problems, the writers of child care manuals were recommending that mothers behave more like fathers – establishing discipline by distantlation.

43. Translated from *Le livret de bébé* (pamphlet) (Villefranche-sur-Saone: Les Etablissements Jacquemaire, n.d.), p. 3.

44. Translated from André Isambert: *Le métier de parents* (Paris: L'Ecole des Parents et des Educateurs, n.d.), p. 13. An accompanying illustration shows both parents holding a watering can over a seated infant holding a flower.

45. For another French use of the "grafting" image – in connection with learning – see quotation on p. 69, below.

46. I am indebted to Geoffrey Gorer for a comment upon these images in terms of French horticultural techniques. In this connection, he also writes:

> "There is … a second type of very elaborate pruning, in which the trees are made to serve a double purpose – architectural as well as horticultural – fruiting trees trained to pyramids, spheres, etc.

> Except for the *espalier,* this is a fairly rare craft, only found on the bigger estates, and demanding a very special skill from the gardeners. But it is specifically French, much as dwarfed, century-old trees in pots are specifically Japanese. Most French people may never have seen such "architectural" fruit gardens; but it is probably an envisaged possibility."

In connection with these nurturing garden metaphors and the image of France as a rural rather than an urban (i. e., agricultural rather than industrial) nation, it is significant that informants' associations to *landscapes* are to those which are primarily man-made – segmented landscapes in which each type of field and wood is cultivated and kept within careful bounds. Grouped together, such images suggest in a circular way the likeness between land which is skillfully nurtured and people who are themselves "formed" as living plants are cultivated.

47. A parallel example of transformation, illustrating how the French conceive of change through development, is provided by Claude Lévi-Strauss's introductory discussion of the incest taboo and the relationship between the biological and social existence of men, when he writes:

> But this union [between the biological and social existence of man through the incest taboo] is neither static nor arbitrary, and at the moment in which it establishes itself, the total situation is modified. In effect, it is less a union than a transformation or a bridge *(passage);* before it, Culture is not yet present *(n'est pas encore donnée* – is not yet given); with it, Nature ceases to exist, for man, as a reigning sovereign. The prohibition of incest is the process by which Nature herself surpasses herself *(la Nature se dépasse elle-même);* she lights the spark through the action of which a structure of a new and more complex type forms itself *(se forme)* and adds itself to *(se superpose),* in integrating them to itself, more simple structures of psychic life, as these latter added themselves to, in integrating to themselves, structures more simple than they, of animal life. It brings about *(opère)* and in itself constitutes the coming of a new order.

Translated from *Les Structures élémentaires de la parenté,* p. 31.

48. An American observer (working in Paris), comparing the handling of American and French infants, emphasizes the "restrictions" to motor development in the case of the French expectations that the child will lie still, sit still, not crawl freely, etc. However, the underlying feeling about restriction is a quite different one for the French than for the American. For the French, it is associated with such praising comments as: *"C'est un enfant sage; il ne bouge du tout"* (That's a good child; he doesn't budge) – which the informant quotes as "a common expression."

49. See also above, p. 20, the quotation describing a desirable infant.

50. Pierre Loti. *The Story of a Child,* translated by Caroline F. Smith, (Boston: C. C. Birchard, 1902), pp. 1, 2.

51. Translated from François Berge, "Editorial," *Chemins du Monde,* No. 1, 1947, pp. 9-10.

52. See, for instance, the methods of teaching advocated by illustration in the recent didactic film, *Passion for Life*. Here traditional teaching (exemplified by the methods of an old schoolmaster and his teacher daughter) is shown to have a stultifying effect upon the children, who, in the classroom, move like mechanical dolls and recite memorized lessons without comprehension. Modern teaching (exemplified by the methods of the young male teacher, a newcomer to the village) enlists the children's own interests in learning what they need to know. However, the teacher himself initiates at every step and, significantly, directs the children to their own parents – a cook, a cobbler, etc. – whose special skills are made the basis of new knowledge for the young generation. Thus, as pictured in this film, new methods revivify what was lost in the old – controlled knowledge based upon models provided by initiating adults.

53. So, for instance, discussing problems encountered in work with French parents and educators, a French child psychologist emphasizes the importance of focusing attention initially upon the needs of the child (rather than upon, say, mother and child as an interesting unit), lest the adults feel "they are to blame" for the child's situation.

54. Lévy-Bruhl's theory of the essential difference between the mental processes of primitive and civilized man (which he himself eventually discarded as erroneous) is one outstanding example of this attitude towards the exotic. In fact, the continuing interest of French anthropologists 'in primitive teleological systems provides numerous examples within the field of social science.

55. Details of actual practices involved in weaning and "habituation" are lacking in our data. Observations of mothers and infants would be required.

56. "French Culture – Preliminary Hypotheses."

57. Ibid.

58. This point was stated very succinctly, in connection with French painting, by Nicolas Calas in a lecture given at the Metropolitan Museum of Art in the spring of 1951.

59. It is apposite that, for the French, the person who is "cold" is someone who does not elicit a response in others (see, for instance, the quotation on p. 11 above describing a woman who did everything in "cold blood"); in contrast, an adjective used to describe a person who is liked – *sympathique* – evokes an idea of responsiveness in which both persons are simultaneously involved. See also the illustration on p. 36 above, where "champagne" becomes a symbol of responsiveness and shared pleasure.

60. See, for instance, Gide's description of his father reading to him as a small child (*If It Die ...* pp. 8-10).

61. Interviewer's summary of informant's account.

62. "French Culture – Preliminary Hypotheses."

63. "The Father Image."

64. In this connection it is interesting to compare French and American versions of jitterbug dancing. Taken over from Americans, the French rein-

terpretations observed (1947) were exceedingly tense and the dance pattern followed by any one couple was tight and limited in its variations.

65. Translated from J. Tronchère: "L'Education sensorielle." *L'Education Enfantine*, Vol. 44, No. 5, January 1950, p. 22.

66. One aspect of this training is reflected in comments by an American mother, who lived for a year in a small French community, that her two young sons "learned such bad language" from their quarrels with French playmates.

67. *The Story of a Child*, pp. 8, 10. These memory images have, of course, a special poignancy in the case of Loti, who spent so much of his adult life in a consciously romantic cultivation of the exotic in the "immense, strange world lying beyond the door."

68. See above, pp. 38-40, for another discussion of this point.

69. Hector Malot's story for children, *Sans Famille* (Paris, 1887, in which two orphans safely recover their family; also such novels as Alain Fournier's *The Wanderer* (*Le Grand Meaulnes,* translated by Françoise Delisle, New York, New Directions Books, 1928); Georges Bernanos' *The Diary of a Country Priest* (translated by Pamela Morris, New York, The Macmillan Co. 1937); François Boyer's *Le jeux inconnus;* François Mauriac's *The Desert of Love* (translated by Gerard Hopkins, New York, Bantam Books, 1952); and so on.

70. Describing the greater freedom of children growing up, or spending summer vacations in a small village, a woman commented that in her village the children could all come and go as they liked during the day because "everyone knew everyone else." For these children the whole village was itself an extension of the *foyer* and the larger family. The village described was also a center of resistance activities during World War II, when the whole village provided for the security and support of the young men as if, it was said, "they all belonged to the village."

71. Martha Wolfenstein: "French Child Training," (an unpublished report of observations made over a two-week period, the summer of 1947. These observations were made previous to organized work by the group studying French culture and were treated by the group in the same way as other data on France seen from a distance.

72. The implications of the use of *tu* and *vous* as forms of address are exceedingly complex and the choice of one or the other may have very different shades of meaning, depending upon the particular context. One example, involving a double reversal, must serve to illustrate the possibilities: Whereas *tu* is, generally speaking, a form of intimate address, in Left political circles it is sometimes used by a whole group to express rebellion against traditional usage. In these circumstances, it is said not to be uncommon for two men who are intimate friends to address each other as tu in formal situations (e. g., at a political meeting) but as *vous* when they are alone, as friends, apart from the group to which they belong.

73. Reticence prevents the use of *ami(e)* in direct reference to a lover or mistress of the same class as the speaker, although it may be used by a third person to refer to someone else's lover or mistress. No unambiguous term

was found to denote a heterosexual friendship; the situation can be handled in such phrases as *"ils sont tres amis"* or *"ils sont tres liés"* (they are very attached), etc., but these too are open to double interpretations. It would seem, indeed, that any modification of *ami* reflects a modification of the form of the total relationship; so, for instance, *un bon ami* (a good friend) is less close to one than *un ami;* the phrase *amitié particulaire* has a homosexual connotation (not necessarily overtly recognized); *amitié amoureuse* describes a very special heterosexual relationship; and so on.

74. We have data only for men on this point. These masculine rivalries are highly specific; vague generalizations made about women (e. g., "all women are potential rivals for some man") do not apply to this masculine situation.

75. According to French informants, members of such concentration camp "families" were capable of acting with great devotion without essentially altering their convictions or personal opinions of one another – thus an individual might be equally condemned for his (or her) views and protected in terms of the immediate situation. This reverses the more usual situation of friendship in which the acceptance of responsibility depends upon a shared viewpoint.

76. See above, Footnote 3, p. 14.

77. It is significant that the French differentiate sharply between those who are opponents *(l'adversaire* is the usual term) and those who are enemies; informants say that *ennemi* is applied (as a political term) *within* France only to those who are opposed to the total system (its application depending, of course, upon the political position of the speaker).

78. The theme of the unsuspected enemy is one that has been treated in a variety of ways by French writers and provides many possibilities of unexpected reversals, including that of the unsuspected *patriot,* i.e., the suspected enemy is a patriot.

79. The image of *le monstre* is applied both to figures outside the *foyer* (cf. discussion of bogeys, above pp. 38–40, 82–84) and to figures within it, e.g., "unnatural" fathers who through greed eat up the children's inheritance or who in naming their heirs prefer strangers to their own family or who take advantage of their legal position to tyrannize their children, and so on. For an example of an evocation of the enemy-stranger as an intruder – "correct" in his daytime appearance, wholly dangerous in his nighttime role – see, for instance, Sartre's sketch, "Paris under the Occupation" (in *French Writing on English Soil,* selected and translated by J. G. Weightman, London, Sylvan Press, 1945, pp. 9-18).

80. Translated from François Berge, "Editorial."

BIBLIOGRAPHY

Adoption. Montevrain (S. -et-M.): Imprimerie de l'Ecole d'Alembert, 1948. (Pamphlet.)

Balzac, Honoré de. *La Cousine Bette.* Paris: Calmann Lévy, 1846.

_____ *Mémoires de deux jeunes mariées.* Paris: Librairie Nouvelle, 1857.

Berge, François. "Editorial." *Chemins du Monde,* No. 1, 1947.

Bernanos, Georges. *The Diary of a Country Priest.* Translated by Pamela Morris. New York: Macmillan Co., 1937.

Boyer, Francois. *Le jeux inconnus.* Paris: Les éditions de minuit, 1947.

Daudet, Alphonse. *Froment jeune et Risler aîné* Paris: Bibliothèque Charpentier, 1928.

Duhamel, Georges. *Chronique des Pasquier.* Paris: Mercure de France, 1933-37.

Fournier, Alain. *The Wanderer.* Translated by Françoise Delisle. New York: New Directions Books, 1928.

Gide, Andre. *If It Die ...* Translated by Dorothy Bussy. London: Secker and Warburg, 1951.

_____. *The School for Wives.* Translated by Dorothy Bussy. New York: Knopf, 1950.

Hanotoux, Gabriel. *Histoire des Colonies Françaises.* Paris: Plon, 1929.

Isambert, Andre. *Le métier de parents.* Paris: L'Ecole de Parents et des Educateurs, n.d.

Jouanneau, L. C., editor. *Discussions du Code Civil dans le Conseil d'E- tat,* 3 vols. Paris, 1805-8.

Lereboullet, P. *Manuel de puériculture,* 5th edition, rev. Paris: Masson, 1949.

Lereboullet, P., and others. *Le guide de la jeune mère,* 8th edition. Paris: Les éditions sociales françaises, 1947.

Lévi-Strauss, Claude. *Les structures élémentaires de la parenté.* Paris: Presses Universitaires de France, 1949.

Le *livret* de *bébé.* Villefranche-sur-Saone: Les établissements Jaque- maire, n.d. (Pamphlet.)

Loti, Pierre. *The Story of a Child.* Translated by Caroline F. Smith. Boston: Birchard, 1902.

McCrary, Tex, and Falkenburg, Jinx. "New York Close-Up." *New York Herald Tribune,* November 23, 1951.

Malot, Hector Henri. *Sans famille.* Paris, 1887.

Martin du Gard, Roger. *Les Thibault.* Paris: Gallimard, 1922-40.

Mauriac, François. *The Desert of Love.* Translated by Gerard Hopkins. New York: Bantam Books, 1952.

Métraux, Rhoda, editor. *Some Hypotheses about French Culture.*
    Columbia University Research in Contemporary Cultures,
    1950. (MSS.)

Petit guide de la jeune maman avant et après la naissance. Paris: Edi-
    tions sociales Françaises, n.d.

Petit Larousse Illustré. Paris: Librairie Larousse, 1908.

Romains, Jules. *Men of Good Will.* New York: Knopf, 1933–46.

Sartre, Jean Paul. "Paris under the Occupation." *In French Writing on
    English Soil.* Selected and translated by J. G. Weightman. Lon-
    don: Sylvan Press, 1945.

Spock, Benjamin. *The Pocket Book of Baby and Child Care.* New York:
    Pocket Books, 1946.

Travaux de la Commission de Réforme du Code Civil, Année 1945-1946.
    Paris: Recueil Sirey, 1947.

Tronchère, J. "L'Education sensorielle." *L'Education Enfantine,* Vol.
    44, No. 5, January 1950.

Vismard, Marcel. *Traité théoretique et pratique de l'adoption et de la
    légitimation adoptive.* Paris: Recueil Sirey, 1951.

Wolfenstein, Martha, and Nathan Leites. *Movies: A Psychological
    Study.* Glencoe, Illinois: Free Press, 1950.

Part Two

THREE BACKGROUND PAPERS

IV. The Family in the French Civil Code:
Adoption and the Tutelle Officeuse

This study of some early 19th-century French attitudes towards the family, with particular reference to adoption, was undertaken with the intention of giving time depth to the attitudes of living French men and women speaking about their own families and family life in general in France today. The study is based on an examination of material selected from one series of documents,[1] *Discussions du Code Civil dans le Conseil* d'Etat,[2] that is, the discussions in 1801–2 by the Conseil d'Etat to whom Bonaparte, as First Consul, had entrusted the task of drawing up a uniform civil code for all of France. For purposes of comparison, brief reference is made also to the discussions of the Civil Code by the Reform Commission in 1945–46.[3] The discussions of the Conseil d'Etat are especially suited to such a study, as they consist of minutes of meetings that are almost verbatim accounts of the proceedings and the speakers are identified individuals who can be placed in the social situation of the time.

In their own lives, the members of the Conseil d'Etat[4] bridged the period from the Monarchy, across the Revolution, to the brief moment of the Consulate. Except for two men (the Marquis de Maleville, whose contributions were considerable, and the Count de Segur, whose apparent influence on the discussions about the family is negligible), all the members of the Conseil were trained lawyers of the higher bourgeoisie; except for one (Tronchet, who was much older), all were men in their middle or late fifties. All had been members of the *Parlement de Paris,* and all had been active in the Revolution but had changed their views during the Terror. Bonaparte, who was then thirty-two, was another exception – and an outsider. As First Consul (Cambacérès, the Second Consul, was chairman), he was often present and participated in the discussions – suggesting, summarizing, and directing the others in their work. In certain respects his viewpoint diverges strikingly from that of the French-born members; where it does, his comments serve to counterpoint French attitudes, highlighting what was common to the thinking of the other participants even when they appeared to be irreconcilably at odds with one another.

Their task was to create a new and harmonious body of law out of the legal systems of the *pays coutumiers* and the *pays de droit écrit* into which the nation had been divided historically. It is significant that the Civil Code survived political change in France for almost one hundred fifty years without major modifications (though with many accretions). And when the Reform Commission first met in 1945, the Minister of Justice stated: "It is not a question of reforming the Civil Code in order to overthrow it, but on the contrary to preserve it."[5] In this the Reform Commission followed tradition, for in the 1801-2 discussions one of the members, Tronchet, had also said: "The drafters of the Civil Code found two systems [of law] established in France ... One must choose between these two systems. And the drafters decided that *in principle the law should disturb the habits of men as little as possible.*[6] Similarly, in 1945-46, when many of the discussions centered on the family, the phrase "maintien de l'esprit familial" (preserve the family spirit) was frequently repeated. This too had clearly been the intention of the members of the Conseil d'Etat in 1801-2. For they made it evident that, however much they disagreed as to the means, they intended to support traditional practice to the extent that this was consistent with safeguarding the state and fortifying the new regime, and to find viable compromises between the conflicting practices of the different regions. So for instance, Maleville (speaking of succession) defended the authority of the father in order to "maintain in families the subordination and the tranquility on which rests the tranquility of the state."[7]

When we turned to this historical material, we had a frame of reference and certain expectations about the order of detail that would be relevant, derived from our study of contemporary French life, particularly of the family. Using the discussions of the Conseil d'Etat as a way of looking backward, we examined them for internal consistencies of attitude in order to see how the results might, in turn, increase our insight into the present. We were, therefore, attempting to work circularly from present to past and back again, looking for congruence (or lack of congruence) in two sets of data over time – combining the historian's methods of handling the source materials of a culture distant in place and time with anthropological methods of deriving statements about a culture from informants. In this presentation, the emphasis is primarily upon the determination of pattern in the historically earlier material.

In the analysis, the discussions of the Conseil d'Etat about the proposed laws concerning adoption and the *tutelle officieuse* (unofficial guardianship) are treated as a unit for, although they are formally different relationships and were separately discussed, the issues raised are closely related.

In these discussions, adoption – as far as the adopter is concerned – involves not only individuals who are members of nuclear family groups, but also those who, perhaps, have no immediate family – no *foyer* – of their own, for adoption is regarded as a means of giving an heir and of passing on a name to those – married or unmarried – *who have no direct heirs*. Adoption does not concern individuals who already have a complete *foyer* in which children are included. The speakers in the Conseil d'Etat make this point – sometimes in negative, sometimes in positive phrasing. In the first draft of the laws on adoption, it was stated negatively: *No person may adopt if he has children or legitimate descendants.*[8]

But a statement that is partly positive was made by a speaker who objected to a suggestion that the right to adopt be limited to married couples:

> It is to know the human heart little, besides, to believe that the power of adopting will one day encourage celibacy, even at an age where the social order invites marriage; nature watches over society and, as one loves one's own children better than those of another, in the same way marriage will not be damaged by adoption. Why, therefore, take away this consolation from men who may often have refrained from marriage only because some infirmity has warned them that that condition is not for them ...[9]

In giving reasons why adoption should be permitted, these are variously phrased as advantages to the person who is to be adopted:

> Adoption shall take place in two cases: one in favor of children to whom the adopter has rendered services during their minority; the other, in favor of persons, even of age, from whom the adopter has himself received important services.[10]

The "important services" referred to were interpreted to mean, for instance, having saved a man's life in battle. More recently, this phrasing has been simplified:

> Adoption can take place only ... if it presents advantages for the adopted persons.[11]

In 1801, it was Bonaparte who, with his somewhat divergent viewpoint, stated the whole position positively, including both members of the adoptive relationship in terms of advantages to each:

> The happy result of adoption will be to give children to those who have been deprived of them, to give a father to children who have been orphans, and finally, to relate old age and virile age to childhood. The transmission of the name is the most natural bond, at the same time that it is the strongest forming this alliance ...

(And outlining the conditions in which adoption might be permitted, he continued:)

Thus, the care that an individual has given to an infant would authorize him to adopt it. The services that he would have received from an adult would give him the same right. There is more; the adoption of an adult would be absurd if it were not motivated by the gratitude of the one who adopts.[12]

Thus, Bonaparte describes a reciprocal relationship and, in doing so, *emphasizes the benefits the adopted person confers on his adopter.* This emphasis is absent from other statements, even those in which both partners (adopter and adopted) are taken into account.

In the eyes of the discussants of 1801, therefore, adoption was a reciprocal relationship in which the advantages to the adopter were somewhat muted, while his wish to do good was stressed, giving the relationship a definitely complementary form – like that (as we shall see) of parent and child, with the difference that what the adopter does of his own volition, the parent does "naturally."

This wish to do good was, however, used as an argument not only by those in favor of, but also by those opposed to adoption. Thus a speaker says:

> *There are, however, other means of doing good,* which do not demand from the one who is their object that he sacrifice his duties and sentiments towards his family ...[13]

What these "other means" might be, was suggested by another speaker:

> Besides, it is not necessary to adopt a child in order to insure its happiness. The faculty of disposing, which will receive even greater latitude, is sufficient. If he [the benefactor] wishes more, he is motivated only by the vanity of perpetuating his name and of leaving the one who is to carry it a considerable fortune in order to maintain the name brilliantly ...[14]

Here the speaker (Tronchet, who steadfastly opposed every measure about adoption but gave some support to proposed measures about the *tutelle officieuse)* clearly separates the desire to benefit a child from considerations of "name" and so, by implication, from the establishment of a family relationship between benefactor and beneficiary.

The *tutelle officieuse,* on the other hand, represented an attempt to create a relationship in which "doing good" was made possible without the strain upon or violation of the *moeurs* which adoption suggested to some of the discussants. This unofficial guardianship defines the relations between a voluntarily protecting adult and a child during its minority, where adoption may or may not be the final intention. The drafted law, as discussed, begins simply:

One who would like to bind an individual to himself legally during the minority of that individual ...[15]

Essentially, unofficial guardianship gave the adult the responsibility of bringing up the child during its minority and, for this purpose, gave him paternal authority and right of consent to marriage; the ward in no sense became a member of the adult's family and did not acquire inheritance or other rights. The very limitations of the *tutelle officieuse,* established between *two individuals* only, created new difficulties in the minds of the discussants, who then – since the ties so created did not extend to other members of the adult's family – asked themselves what would become of the child if the protecting adult should die during the child's minority while its education – which the adult had undertaken – was still incomplete. It is significant that the makers of the Civil Code discussed the problem of the *tutelle officieuse* very energetically and felt it advisable to give legal sanction to a relationship intermediate between mere benefaction to someone outside the close family and the incorporation of the outsider, in however limited a way, in the most intimate relationship system.[16]

A consistently expressed feeling in these discussions was that once a relationship (such as adoption) had been established, it could neither be wiped out nor altered by *reversal,* although it might alter with changing circumstances. So, in adoption the question was raised whether a child was owed an indemnity if, when it reached majority, the prospective adopter changed his mind and did not wish to consummate the adoption for which he had declared himself ready when he took charge of the child. (In the drafts and in the law as it first stood, adoption could be consummated only when the ward reached its majority and could speak in its own behalf. The age when this could be done, legally, has dropped steadily.) Then, too, what would happen to such a child if it were obliged to return to its true family ?

A vivid illustration of the effect of such a change in outer circumstance is given by a speaker who was not in favor of adoption:

> Besides, the [adopting] father often opens the way for regrets, the more violent because they are without remedy. A couple have no children. One of them dies. The other remarries. There are children. One can easily imagine the regrets in having given them a stranger for a brother. This is where one sees how far adoption is from imitating nature. Hatred will spring up between the father and the adopted son, between the latter and the natural children; from it will come discord which will trouble the entire family for along time ...[17]

Of the return of the adopted child to its own family (after the death of the prospective adopter), the speaker goes on to say:

What will he [the child] find there? Misery. *For his return, undoubtedly, will not change anything retroactively* in the division and other disposals upon which rests the fortune of his brothers.[18]

The same point of irreversibility, even when circumstances have changed, is made in connection with education and the problem of how to provide for a child – whether it is perhaps owed an indemnity – when the *tuteur officieux* or prospective adopter has died without making a testamentary declaration. Arguing that foreknowledge of such an indemnity under these circumstances would reassure a father who was about to give up a child in adoption, a speaker says:

> Paternal tenderness should [make the father] foresee that a child who, having received a brilliant education, should be reduced to finding his subsistence in hard and painful work, would remain without resources and maybe would be reduced to finding them through unlawful means ...[19]

Another speaker makes the same point even more forcefully when he contrasts different types of education and the different obligations arising from them:

> He who has given to the child a brilliant and distinguished education seems to have undertaken the obligation of leaving him at least an allowance; this has always been the opinion of the courts. It is not by his choice that the child has emerged from the simplicity of his original state and has been made incapable of rude and painful work. The allowance can therefore only be refused if he has received an ordinary education and when he has learned a trade.[20]

This was said in reply to a comment by Bonaparte that the most owing to a child would be that it be cared for until it had reached an age when it could support itself – fifteen or sixteen years.

In both these instances it is the child who has been irreversibly altered by the processes of education. There is here, in fact, a triply weighted argument: In addition to the point of irreversibly, it is argued that he who has paternal authority must provide for a child (plan for its future) and that appropriate action must be based upon appropriate preparation. These latter arguments are based on an assumption that the child is formed by *what is done to it.*

In discussing such hypothetical cases, speakers both assume that people act in ways that are reasonable and "natural," *and* take account of the fact that some – because of their character or special circumstances in which they find themselves – may be expected to behave badly. At the same time they argue that the "unnatural" and unreasonable instances are rare and that the laws cannot be made primarily with them in mind. Thus, speaking of a situation in which the *ward*, on coming of age, might refuse adoption, one man asked – and answered himself:

> But it is said [the child's] refusal can be determined by the bad behavior of the adopter. *Such a reason will always be very rare:* the most general reason for the refusal by the child will be his attachment to his family [of birth].[21]

Another man, questioning whether the law should establish "an absolute rule" about the payment of indemnities, asked "why everything should be put to whim and nothing to reason?"[22]

This swing between dependence upon the normal to control situations and concern for the abnormal situation is a recurrent one in discussions of various subjects. So, for instance, considering problems related to paternal authority, the question is raised to what extent the father's sole and unqualified right to have his minor son put in a reformatory should be supported or should be modified by consultation. Explaining a proposed article, a speaker said:

> [The article] is based upon the *justified assumption that the father will use his authority only because of affection for the child and for the child's good;* that he will act only to put back on an honorable road, without spoiling it, a child whom he loves, but whom this tenderness forces him to punish. *This will indeed be the most ordinary case, the one, consequently, which the law must conjecture* ...[23]

However, a less optimistic speaker cast some doubt upon the possible motives of the father:

> Generally the mistakes of the children are the result of the weaknesses, the thoughtlessness, or the bad examples of the fathers; *these do not deserve, therefore, absolute confidence* ...[24]

A third speaker added to this doubt:

> Whatever confidence fathers deserve, the law should not be based upon the false assumption that all are equally good and virtuous. The law should hold the scales with equity and not forget that hard laws often prepare revolutions ...[25]

A fourth speaker then concluded:

> Prudence demands that one should beware of passions; now fathers have no less than other men ...[26]

Similar arguments were used to support or to oppose proposed measures concerning succession and inheritance. Speaking in favor of regulating the father's authority to dispose, one member said (in connection with substitutions):

> One could not do better, without doubt [than to leave everything up to the father] if all men were animated by generous sentiments and moved by justice. *But as it is also in the nature of man to be accessible to predelictions, prejudices, vanity and hatred and a host of unruly passions,* the law has to interpose itself between even the father and the children ...[27]

Another man, however, who felt that the father should be given the greatest possible latitude in disposal, remarked in a later discussion:

> *What unnatural father, abusing the latitude given to him under the law* for a different purpose, would give half his fortune to a stranger ... *the law does not presuppose monsters; it does not make statutes for such extraordinary events.*[28]

Formal adoption, as it was being considered by the Conseil d'Etat in 1801, was a new institution without clear French precedents upon which rules might be established, although all had Roman law in their minds as a model. This is undoubtedly why so much heated debate and opposition developed around this problem. Thus, some speakers said that adoption was antithetical to French custom; one even regarded it as "immoral." Another fundamental issue was raised in a discussion about the transmission of names:

> Names are a property of the family; they cannot be changed arbitrarily without *bringing great confusion to society* ...[29]

(This is a retort to a comment by Bonaparte that the transmission of the name is a principal effect of adoption.) In fact, the question of whether and how this "great confusion to society" was to be avoided or overcome was implicit in much of the lengthy discussion. So, for example, when the first drafts of the laws on adoption were being considered, while the ostensible problem was the means by which adoption was to be accomplished (i. e., by legislative act or by authority of the courts), the speakers returned continually to the principles involved. Similarly, in considering proposed laws about the *tutelle officieuse,* the speakers again took up problems essentially related to adoption. And even those who supported the idea of adoption seemed to feel that there were almost insuperable difficulties of execution.

Essentially, these difficulties were of four kinds: (1) those concerning the relationship of the child to its family of birth, on the one hand, and to its adoptive family, on the other; and, related to this, (2) the relationship of those family members not directly involved in the adoption to the child and to one another; (3) the confusions arising from a mixed voluntary and "natural" relationship; and, partly related to this, (4) the problem of limiting the spread of the "great confusion." We may take these up in turn.

Generally speaking, the members of the Conseil d'Etat (with the exception of Bonaparte) tended to assume that the child who was to be adopted had a complete *living* family, both parents and siblings. Except quite formally, they did not refer to *orphans*. Thus, one man speaking against the whole idea of adoption said:

> It places the child between fortune and abandoning its parents ...[30]

Another, replying to this point, said:

> Besides, [adoption] cannot have the immoral consequences which have been ascribed to it; for, *far from obliging the adopted child to renounce the affection which he owes to his natural father,* the adoption facilitates, on the contrary, the means of helping this father in his misfortunes.[31]

Still another remarked (in connection with a discussion of indemnities):

> The law should not sanction ..., the type of sale *a father will make of his child* ...[32]

In the same discussion, another commented:

> *The father who abandons his son to a stranger* is no more worthy of esteem than the *one who would sell him* ...[33]

It is clear that both those who favored and those who opposed the payment of an indemnity, for example, referred to a *living father* who gave his child in adoption.

The presumption that the child also had siblings has already been referred to in the discussion of what happened when an adopted child returned to its family of origin:

> For his return, undoubtedly, will not change anything retroactively in the division and other disposals upon which rests the fortune *of his brothers.*[34]

The assumption that there is a living family is reflected in the laws themselves (although provision is also made in them for foundlings and orphans):

No legitimate child may be offered for adoption *except by its* father *and mother, or by one of the survivors* if the other is dead.

All other relatives, even the ascendants, may not *instead of the mother and the father* offer the child for adoption, unless it has been legally established that it is without means of subsistence.[35]

In the laws, the assumption of a living family has continued up to the present, for in the modern Civil Code the statement stands:

The obligation to furnish nourishment continues to exist between the *adopted and his mother and father* ...[36]

In the discussions of the Conseil d'Etat, Bonaparte was the one who criticized this preoccupation with the child's own family and is the only one who insisted otherwise:

The question is not being faced as it should be. Adoption is absurd if one supposes that *it brings face to face two fathers, one natural and the other adoptive, to discuss together a child.* Adoption is principally established in order *to give a father to orphans in the form of individuals who, having only distant heirs, would like to bind themselves to a child* ... Therefore it is hampering the discussion if one centers it around the rare and less favorable cases where motives of interest determine the father to give his son into adoption ...[37]

According to the laws, as first proposed for discussion, the child entirely gave up its relationship to its family of birth and became, in the full sense, a member of its adopter's family. This, however, created special difficulties even as it solved others. Thus, a speaker points out:

The introduction of the adopted child into the family of the adopting person, making the relatives of the first into the relatives of the second, without their formal consent, not even with their tacit consent, *is difficult to reconcile with our ideas and our customs. The fiction extended beyond the contracting parties is carrying things too far.*[38]

And, a little later in the discussion, another man said:

The adopted child will have rights only on the goods of the adopter? *Then the child becomes in society a monstrous being; he is cut off from his own family and yet he does not belong to his adoptive family.* Will he have all the rights of natural children? In that case the legislator is unjust towards *the relatives of the foster father* and more liberal than he has a right to be; for it is not within his province to take away from the citizen the right of succession, which is for him a real property in all the degrees that it covers.[39]

Finally, through a series of compromises, adoption was set up as a relationship exclusively between two persons (or three when spouses adopted conjointly), entered into, as a rule, during the minority of the person to be adopted but consummated only when the child attained majority or, under certain conditions, by testamentary declaration at the death of the adopter. The adopted child still retained rights in and duties towards its family of birth, and it acquired only certain rights in relation to its adopter.

Nevertheless, the crucial problem of the handling of family properties seems never to have been solved entirely satisfactorily, nor was the problem of the obligations of relatives of the adopting person to the one adopted fully worked out. The individual who is not born into a family may be regarded as a "stranger" when questions of family property arise.

Essentially and in spite of the fact that the adopter was given paternal authority over the ward, adoption established a relationship that was, during the child's minority, a *voluntary* one. That is, final adoption could not take place until the child could speak in its own right. While its natural protectors could put it into the care of another person, thereby giving their own consent to a severance of ties, they could not break the bond between themselves and the child or create a bond between the child and anyone else in the child's name. The new relationship could be validated only by adopter and adopted.

The importance of free, voluntary relationships is stressed in several connections, as when a speaker said:

> There is a lot of [informal] adoption going on in the country and it is successful. Why? Because *it binds neither the one who adopts nor the one adopted, because each remains entirely free.* The [adopting] father knows that if the gratitude of the [adopted] son ceases, the favor ceases also; the son knows that the father is not pledged; this knowledge keeps him within his duty ...[40]

The issue of voluntary action is raised also by the members of the Conseil who opposed the payment to the child of an indemnity under certain conditions. One speaker said:

> The more conditions there will be imposed on generous acts, the rarer they will get ...[41]

Another added:

> Never has a good deed imposed the obligation of another good deed ...[42]

And later in the same discussion, the same speaker remarked:

> The law should neither require a declaration nor speak of a contract; it should give free play to affection on the one side, gratitude on the other.[43]

Nevertheless, he went on to say, invoking the duty usually attributed as natural to a parent (and therefore, in fact, shifting his position):

> If later one should take advantage of the silence of this law [with regard to the payment of an indemnity] to refuse a child the allowance he had a right to hope for, he would have recourse to the courts who would award it to him, basing themselves on the principle that the care which was taken of him carries with it the obligation to feed him to a certain age.[43]

Another speaker, picking up the contradiction in this statement, used the same point of voluntary action in an opposite sense:

> It is doubtful that the courts will condemn a citizen to furnish an allowance to a child until his majority only because he did it for some time, but without any preliminary obligation on his side; the essence of a good deed is that it should be entirely free and its extent should depend upon the will of the author; it requires very extraordinary circumstances to oblige the courts to deviate from the first principle.[44]

The effect of constraint and regulation upon such a voluntary relationship was most succinctly stated by a speaker who opposed adoption because, comparing it to the relationship of parent and child, adoption could never be "anything but a very imperfect image of nature." He then continued:

> There is more: [adoption] will destroy the affections which are the bonds [of nature] because it destroys their independence and changes them into duties. Man is naturally the enemy of constraint; he wants to be free even in the acts which are dictated by sentiment ...[45]

Thus, in such a voluntary relationship of choice, the strength of the tie seems to derive from the absence of external regulation and of the sense of obligation. It is exactly this freely chosen desire to do good to a child that was stressed in the discussions of adoption and the *tutelle officieuse*. But in the plan, according to which adoption or even the decision to adopt was postponed until the child was able to give its consent, there is an inherent instability, and it was precisely in regard to this that difficulties arose in the minds of the discussants.

Within the *foyer,* in the relationships into which the individual is born, the emotions are, so to speak, given. Again and again speakers assume that because an individual is a father or a son or a daughter, he or she will have certain emotions as a matter of course. The emotions of parent and child, for example, are different but are matched. No choice is assumed in the emotions felt in these familial relationships, although it is recognized that not all individuals do feel the appropriate emotions or that these may be overridden by "passions" and the like. (See above, the quotations on pp. 74-75.)

In both types of relationship – those established by birth and those entered into voluntarily – the emotions are conceived of as "natural" and, for the most part, spontaneous; in both, what is felt may alter – with accompanying changes in behavior – through disturbances. In a voluntary relationship the disturbance may be, as was suggested in the passage quoted, the loss of the element of choice; in family relationships incorrect behavior is a source of disturbance – as when a father introduces a "stranger" into the *foyer* ("One can easily imagine the regrets at having given them a stranger for a brother. This is where one will see how far adoption is from imitating nature" etc.[46]), or when an "unnatural father ... would give half his fortune to a stranger."[47]

In connection with adoption, there are references to various *familial* emotions: the attachment of the child to its family of birth; the "paternal tenderness" that might cause a father to demand a guaranty before giving up his child, as well as his "deep affection" and "desire to be useful" that might lead him to give up the child; the "devotion and tenderness which [a father] has a right to expect from a real child" but which the foster father "will never find." In connection with adoption and the collaterals' rights of succession, there are references to "an order of natural affections" in which

> The first degree, without doubt, belongs to the children; yet nature also speaks in favor of brother and sister, in favor of nephews who are, in a way, children ...[48]

There appears to be a doubt in the minds of the speakers that adopter and adopted can continuously and in spite of changing circumstances feel the emotions ascribed to the parent-child *situation*. Adoption is, in fact, a mixed relationship with elements both of choice and of the given, and this seems to be, in part at least, the source of the sense of instability that disturbed not only those opposed to but also those in favor of adoption.

As a relationship of choice, adoption (after the rejection of the laws first proposed by which the child became wholly a member of the adopter's family) is essentially limited to the two individuals directly concerned; other persons do not, because of their ties to the one, enter into relations with the other partner. In this relationship of choice, the emotions felt arise from behavior and mutual interest, rather than being derived from the relationship itself.

Yet, as a relationship, adoption is fixed; that is, it is subject to external regulation. The protecting adult has regulative powers (paternal authority, consent to marriage) and duties in which he is assimi-lated to a parent (the duty of providing nourishment, of educating the ward). Like that of parent and child, the relationship is a complemen-tary one with particular emphasis upon what is done for the child (and the benefits to the adopter are muted – except by Bonaparte).

The mixed nature of the relationship, as they saw it, was one of the main difficulties that hindered the members of the Conseil d'Etat in arriving at a full definition of adoption. Both in arguments for and against various regulations, the pattern of choice is opposed to the pattern of the family with its fixed relationships, the discussion shift-ing now in the one, now in the other direction in its emphasis. This is particularly clear in the discussion of what was owing to a ward if the protecting adult should die or should not fulfill the expectation to adopt. Since participation in the relationship was limited to the two individuals, it was felt, on the one hand, that the natural heirs of the adult had no obligations towards the child. But, since the adult had undertaken the care of the child, it was felt, on the other hand, that the adult owed the child a father's obligatory education and preparation for adult life. Yet it was argued that if the child were promised an indemnity (if the obligations were not fulfilled), the adult's care was no longer a free deed of good will. And if failure were not provided for in advance, upon whom (and for what reason) would the obligation fall? The important arguments on this point have already been quoted.

This discussion particularly indicates how the two sorts of rela-tionship – established by birth or by choice – were opposed. In addition, the need to avoid confusion, to clarify by reconciling fact and principle in a new definition and by compartmentalization is emphasized. When the situation cannot be defined, when the compartmentalization breaks down, the result is confusion to society: the child without a defined family is a "monster"; the adopted child, compared to natural children, is a "stranger." The altered situation cannot be reversed.

In the discussion of the adoption laws in 1801-2, as well as in the development of the laws since that time, there has been a consistent effort made to limit the area of the confusion, that is, to prevent the initial and inevitable confusions from spreading.

Thus, for example, according to the first draft of the adoption laws, only marriage partners could adopt conjointly and only true sib-lings of the originally adopted child could be adopted by the same per-son (or by the marriage partners) during the lifetime of the child or of the child's descendants. This meant, in effect, that only one family group could enter into an adoptive relationship with a particular child and also that only the children from one family could be brought into an adoptive relationship to one another. It automatically limited the number of families that could be made into "fictitious" relatives.[49]

In the discussions of the Conseil d'Etat, the question was raised as to whether nephews who "are in a way children" could not be exempted from the general regulations about adoption and, in the first draft of the laws, specific exemptions were proposed. However, this proposal was rejected on the grounds that it would interfere with the laws of succession and would give unfair advantage to one of a whole class of collateral relatives, thus creating endless friction.[50]

(Similarly, in the present Civil Code – up to 1939 – there are specific regulations prohibiting the marriage of the adopter or of the ward to certain persons related to each.[51] This again may be seen as an attempt to limit the extent of the confusion of relationships. It is noteworthy, however, that prohibitions against the marriage of an adopted and a true child could be removed "for serious reasons.")

The discussions of the Conseil d'Etat and the articles of law worked out by them and by others from that time to the present in the matter of inheritance likewise illustrate the concern for clarification and limitation. The solutions originally arrived at established a balanced compromise depending upon three more or less fixed elements: the relationship of the protecting adult and the ward, and the relationship of each of these to his own family of birth. It is of special interest to us here that the descendants of the ward follow the lines of the relationship between the ward and the adopter and also between the ward and the ward's family of birth, but exclude totally other family members of the adopting person. The rights of the adopting person in inheritance from his ward, however, are entirely limited to those goods which he himself has given the ward.

It is evident from this as from other discussions, that the members of the Conseil d'Etat had a positive attitude towards the rights of collaterals as members of a family group. (See especially quotations above, pp. 77 and 80.) Their attitude is highlighted by Bonaparte's markedly different one, which he expressed in the following:

> One can, therefore, oppose to adoption only the despair of the collaterals. This result will undoubtedly not be put among the number of inconveniences; the interest of the collaterals is nothing, and even, if one calculates well, one will find that it is treated better in an adoption than in an unconditional donation of property; for the conformity of name establishes between them and the adopted relations which, in various circumstances, can be advantageous to them.[52]

These discussions make clear how important it seemed to the speakers to keep whatever belonged to a family intact in that family and, as far as possible, out of the reach of an outsider.

Similarly, the protection of the father's right to conserve his fortune for himself and his family as he saw fit was a factor in the rejection of the proposed law that would have permitted a daughter to demand a dowry. A possible situation is pictured:

> In the regions of written law a daughter may ask a dowry even after she is married; and then she is under the influence of her husband who, naturally, does not have towards the father the same tenderness, the same respect as the daughter. As a result, an interested man could marry a girl without a dowry in the hope of demanding it later from the father, whom he would pursue in the name of the daughter without regard ...[53]

And likewise, in the discussion of ordinary guardianship over children, giving this office to the widow was opposed because she might remarry and then the control of her deceased husband's properties would fall into the hands of an outsider:

> There exists between the father and the mother a difference that must not be lost sight of. The father, when he remarries, remains the master of his affairs; he needs only himself to administer the property of his children; the mother, on the other hand, when she remarries, ceases to belong to herself. Thus, if the guardianship is left to her, it would be proper to make her husband responsible [an unthinkable solution].[54]

The point is made even more clearly by the next speaker, who added:

> It is not just to confuse the father and the mother, for the marriage of the father does not change the state of the family; it always keeps the same head, *while the remarried mother passes into another family and under the authority of her second husband.*[55]

Thus the specific problem, whether it concerns the relations of a ward to its adopter and his family or to its own family of birth, or the duties of a father to his married daughter who now belongs to another family, or the ability of a widow who remarries to administer her children's inheritance from a father to whose family she no longer belongs, and so on, and whether an individual supports one or another position with respect to a solution, can be best understood in terms of a particular family structure and a way of handling structured situations so as to "avoid confusion" that is common to all of them. In the discussions of the Conseil d'Etat, the attitudes of Bonaparte provide contrast against which those of the French members can be seen as wholly congruent.

A single detail may serve here to suggest the stability of the pattern (but the reversibility of the *content* of that pattern) over time. In 1801-2, the Conseil rejected the proposal that the adopted individual become a full member of the adopter's family; he remained instead within his own family but had rights and obligations with respect to his adopter as an individual. In 1939, an alternative decree, *permitting* the ward to become a full member of the adopting family was welcomed with enthusiasm:

> Later the law of July 29, 1939 gave to married couples without posterity the possibility of tying to themselves children *whose status became the same as that of legitimate children.* The adoptive legislation thus created was immediately received with great favor and it is under veritable pressure of public opinion ...[56]

It is still only "married couples without posterity" who can adopt. The reasons for the change of regulation and for the favor with which it was received would have to be the subject of another sort of investigation. The common element here and in the discussions of the Conseil d'Etat and of the Reform Commission is concern for the place of the individual in a family system, the definition of which is shared.

NOTES

1. The study of the *Discussions* centered on sections of the proposed laws that concerned marriage (but not forms of marriage contract), the dowry, paternity and filiation, paternal authority, adoption, the *tutelle officieuse* (unofficial guardianship), guardianship and emancipation, interdiction, and succession. As the documentary material turned out to be an exceedingly rich source requiring extended analysis, the present study concentrates on the sections on adoption and the *tutelle officieuse* with occasional quotations from other sections. The background work and the selection and translation of materials from the meetings of the Conseil d'Etat were done by Nelly Hoyt. Selections from the discussions of the Reform Commission were made for comparison by Rhoda Métraux.

2. L. C. Jouanneau, editor, 1805-8.

3. *Travaux de la Commission de Réforme du Code Civil, Annie 1945-1946*, 1947.

4. The members of the Conseil d'Etat were: Cambacérès (Chairman), Berlier, Bigot-Preameneu, Jollivet, Lebrun, Maleville, Real, Regnaud, Segur, Thibaudeau, Treilhard, and Tronchet.

5. *Travaux* ... , p. 21.

6. Jouanneau, *op. cit.*, Vol. I, p. 297. *(Italics throughout are the writers'.)*

7. *Ibid.*, Vol..II, p. 134.

8. Jouanneau, *op. cit.*, Vol. I, p. 440. This qualification has been maintained up to the present (1939).

9. *Ibid.*, p. 455. Berlier was speaking here of the various qualifications for adoption (on the part of the adopter), including age.

    The qualifications of the adopter remain an issue today and the question is raised now – as in the past – whether the person who wishes to adopt may not have a legitimate child at some later time. In 1945, in connection with cases where sterility is presumed, the situation is positively phrased:

    > Finally one must note that, to permit the adopter without descendants to assure the survival of his name and the devolution of his succession... (*Travaux ...* , p. 543).

10. Jouanneau, *op. cit.*, Vol. I, p. 452. This is Article I of the second draft of laws on adoption.

11. H. Crachard, 1930, p. 122. This is Article 343 of the Civil Code (before 1939).

12. Jouanneau, *op. cit.*, Vol. I, p. 451.

13. Ibid., p. 445. The speaker, Bigot-Preameneu, considered that adoption was, for the reason given, "immoral."

14. *Ibid.*, p. 448. In this statement there is indirect reference to the earlier situation when the nobility, by letters of patent, could confer their name on a designated heir. Although this was one of the few precedents for adoption in France, it was one that was unacceptable to those who had taken part in the Revolution and who wished to break with all that might support the nobility.

    The "faculty of disposing" to which the speaker refers, was itself the subject of heated debate in which one of the main questions was the degree of latitude a man should be permitted to dispose of property outside the immediate family. Thus, while the right of disposal was given as a possible alternative to adoption (to keep the family intact), limitation of the right of disposal was sought by some (to keep the family intact). Considerations of the family are central in both situations.

15. *Ibid.*, p. 465.

16. Yet a French informant, a lawyer, commented that this is a legal tie seldom used nowadays. No investigation of the question was made.

17. Jouanneau, *op. cit.*, Vol. I, p. 448. The speaker is Tronchet.

18. *Ibid.* A related point, though with another emphasis, is made by a speaker in the 1945 discussions (*Travaux ...* , pp. 563-64), when he says:

    > If the adopters die, are placed under interdiction or disappear during the minority of the adopted, the latter falls back under the paternal authority of his own ascendants (*ascendants d'origine*). This solution seems to us detestable. This intervention of the original family ... can lead to very bad results. In particular, the blood *ascendants are little qualified* to administer the fortune which the minor has inherited from his relatives by adoption ... In the situation foreseen by the speaker in 1801, the family is unable to return to conditions that

existed before the child had been taken to be adopted, even though the child (the speaker says) returned of its own accord by refusing adoption. In the situation foreseen by the speaker in 1945, the family is unable to adjust itself to the changed circumstances of the child who has been adopted but who has now returned to them enriched. There is in common in the two cases an assumption of inability to adjust retroactively when a change once has been made.

19. Jouanneau, *op. cit.*, Vol. I, p. 473.

20. *Ibid.* The speaker is Treilhard.

21. *Ibid.* Vol. I, p. 471. A statement by Bigot-Preameneu.

22. *Ibid.* A point made by Cambacérès, the Second Consul, who is supporting the reasonableness with which individuals may be expected to act.

23. *Ibid.*, p. 489. It is again Bigot-Preameneu who speaks here.

24. *Ibid.*, p. 490. A statement by Treilhard.

25. *Ibid.* Cambacérès here reverses his position (see Note 21 above).

26. *Ibid.*, p. 491. A statement by Lebrun.

27. *Ibid.*, Vol. II, p. 104. A statement by Thibaudeau.

28. *Ibid.*, p. 133. A statement by the Marquis de Maleville.

29. *Ibid*, p. 445. A statement by Treilhard.

30. *Ibid.*, p. 446. The speaker is Bigot-Preameneu, who considered adoption immoral.

31. *Ibid.*, p. 446. A statement by Regnaud

32. *Ibid.*, p. 472. The speaker is Tronchet

33. *Ibid.*, p. 473. The speaker is Real.

34. *Ibid.*, p. 448. The speaker is Tronchet. See also Note 17.

35. *Ibid.*, p. 440. These two statements appear as Articles IX and X in the original draft of laws concerning adoption.

36. Cachard, *op cit.*, p. 124. The statement is taken from Article 356 of the Civil Code. Preoccupations with the family of the child that is to be given in adoption have continued up to the present. For example, in the course of long deliberations by the Reform Commission about consent to adoption, after considering various situations in which *living parents* (one of whom might be absent, missing, etc.) might be involved, the situation is discussed in which both parents are dead or away and then questions are raised about the rights of consent of the *grandparents* when the orphaned child is in their care. Thus, having acknowledged tile possibility that parents may be absent or dead, it is then assumed that the child nevertheless has living relatives – has a family – in the next ascending generation. (*Travaux* … , p. 614 ff.)

37. Jouanneau, *op. cit.*, Vol. I, p. 473. Bonaparte here again stresses the reciprocal need of both persons in tile adoptive relationship.

38. *Ibid.*, p. 443. Berlier is here summarizing objections to adoption.

39. *Ibid.*, p. 449. A statement by Tronchet.

40. *Ibid.*, p. 448. The speaker is Tronchet.

41. *Ibid.*, p. 468. The speaker is Jollivet.

42. *Ibid.* The speaker is Bigot-Preameneu.

43. *Ibid.*, p. 476.

44. *Ibid.*, p. 477. The speaker is the Marquis de Maleville.

45. *Ibid.*, p. 447. The speaker is Tronchet.

46. *Ibid.*, p. 448. A statement, already quoted, by Tronchet.

47. *Ibid.*, Vol. II, p. 133. A statement, already quoted, by the Marquis de Maleville.

48. *Ibid.*, Vol. I, p. 451. The speaker is Tronchet.

49. *Ibid.*, p. 440. See Articles V and VII of the proposed laws. The regulation that only a married couple can adopt conjointly has been maintained up to the present in essentially unaltered form. See Article 346 of the Civil Code. Cachard, *op. cit.*, p. 122.

50. Jouanneau, *op. cit.*, Vol. I, p. 440, the proposed Article VI; pp. 451-52, discussions of the proposal.

51. Cachard, *op. cit.*, p. 124. Articles 354 and 355 of the Civil Code.

52. Jouanneau, *op. cit.*, Vol. I, p. 450. It is interesting to notice here that in trying to make a formal compromise with his listeners, Bonaparte selected as a point of concession one about which they were certain to disagree with him – the value of the relations between the ward and the adopter's collaterals.

53. *Ibid.*, p. 302. It is Regnaud's account.

54. *Ibid.*, p. 502. The speaker is Bigot-Preameneu.

55. *Ibid.*, p. 503. Cambacérès is the speaker.

56. From a report by Henry Molinar, "Adoption et légitimation adoptive" in *Travaux ... ,* p. 542.

BIBLIOGRAPHY

Henry Cachard, editor. *The French Civil Code,* revised edition. Paris and London: The Lecram Press, 1930.

Henri Capitant. *L'évolution du droit de la famille depuis le code civil.* Montreal: Barreau, 1936.

Code Civil. Annoté d'après la doctrine et la jurisprudence. Paris: Librairie Dalloz, 1949.

Paul Coste-Floret. *La nature juridique du droit de propriété d'après le code civil et depuis le code civil.* Paris: Recueil Sirey, 1935.

L. C. Jouanneau, editor. *Discussions du Code Civil dans le Conseil d'E-tat,* 3 volumes. Paris, 1805-8.

Henri Lavedan. *La famille Française.* Paris: Perrin, 1917.

J. C. Locre. *Esprit du Code Napoleon,* 7 volumes. L'Imprimerie Impéri-ale, 1807-14.

Gabriel d'Olivier. *Observations sur le code civil.* Paris: Carpentras, 1807.

Maurice Picard. "L'évolution du régime des biens depuis le code civil." *Le droit civil français.* Paris: In Bar of Montreal, 1936.

J. E. M. Portalis. *Discours rapports et travaux inédits sur le code civil.* Paris, 1844.

Jean Ray. *Essai sur la structure logique du code civil français.* Paris: Alcan, 1926.

_____. *Index du code civil.* Paris: Alcan, 1936.

René Roblot. *Code civil et principaux textes complementaires.* Paris: Librairie générale de droit et de jurisprudence, 1946.

_____. *Code de la famille.* (Les lois françaises à la portée de tous.) Paris, 1920.

Travaux de la Commission de Réforme du Code Civil, Annie 1945-1946. Paris: Recueil Sirey, 1947.

V. Plot and Character in Selected French Films: An Analysis of Fantasy

The films of a particular culture, as well as its literature, tend to express the course and consequences of human emotions and relationships in a characteristic way. We have looked in French films for recurrent patterns of plot and character; such recurrences, which would seem to be not wholly intended, appear to reflect feelings and attitudes typical of the culture. By typical we do not mean that they prevail without exception nor that they have no existence elsewhere. Nor do we expect to find in films or other fantasy productions an exact replica of real life behavior. There is rather a complex interplay between actual life and the wishes and fears which it fulfills or denies.

For this analysis we have examined some forty French films, mainly produced since the middle 1930's. Our judgment as to what is distinctive in them is based on a fairly extensive comparison with contemporary American and British films.*

Our analysis of French films begins with the dominant figure of the father, who tends, more often than a son figure, to bear the role of the suffering hero. We proceed to a consideration of the hazards to which human impulses are seen as exposing us, and the unreliability of justice. Finally, we discuss some of the major disappointing experiences with which French films are preoccupied.

The Father as Suffering Hero

One of the major creations of French films is the sympathetic father figure, who very often is a dominant character. He frequently falls in love with a daughter figure and obstructs the happiness of a son figure. His ability to obstruct is, however, mitigated by awareness of his age and his declining powers. Where the obstructiveness of the father figure is most pronounced, there is the most explicit acknowledgment of his weakness and imminent death. In *Farrebique,* the old father postpones as long as possible turning over the family farm to his older son, and arranges the marriage of the younger son only on his death bed. The whole film elaborates the disappointments of the old man in his last year of life, especially his failure to realize his dream of rebuilding the house, and ends with his death. In *Le Corbeau,* an exceptionally destructive father figure attacks a younger col-

---

* Wolfenstein, Martha and Leites, Nathan. *Movies: A Psychological Study.* Glenco, Illinois: Free Press, 1950.

league with whom his wife has fallen in love; the older man is the impotent husband of the beautiful young woman.

French films dramatize the conflict between paternal and erotic impulses in the aging man, especially the reversion from the paternal to the erotic which is apt to be precipitated in relation to a maturing daughter figure. Where the erotic tendency becomes predominant, the result is tragic. In *Symphonie Pastorale,* the aging pastor falls in love with his adopted daughter, a beautiful blind girl, whom he has cared for and educated from her childhood. When her sight is restored by an operation, she is disillusioned to see that the pastor is an old man, and turns to his son who also loves her. The father drives the son away and the girl commits suicide. In *Les Visiteurs du Soir,* a feudal lord is about to celebrate the marriage of his daughter to a young noble with whom he is on the most friendly terms. Two emissaries of the devil, a handsome young man and a woman disguised as minstrels, arrive at the castle. Their function is to release the erotic impulses which are aroused in the father by the prospect of his daughter's marriage, as well as his latent jealous hostility towards his prospective son-in-law. The demonic woman, a sinister counterpart of the daughter, induces both the father and the son-in-law to make love to her. They then fight a duel over her in which the father kills the younger man. The demonic young man, an alternate to the son-in-law, makes love to the daughter, and the father has him chained up in a dungeon, thus doubling his vengeance against the son-in-law. Eventually the devil, who may be regarded as representing the malign aspect of the father, turns the daughter and her lover to stone.

Where the paternal impulse triumphs over the erotic, the distinctive resigned tragicomic father figure (typically Raimu) appears. In *La Fille du Puisatier,* the father plans to satisfy his love for his maturing oldest daughter vicariously by marrying her to his assistant. He defends himself against his attraction towards her by reviving memories of the more fullsome charms of her dead mother. When the daughter is about to have an illegitimate child, he drives her from the house, his anger and grief at her unfaithfulness being well cloaked by conventional indignation. When he learns that she has borne a son (his wife had given him only daughters) and that the child will bear his name, and when he sees the child, he is overwhelmed by paternal feelings and brings the daughter and baby back home with him. In *Fanny,* the aging man is delighted to give his name to the child of the young woman by another man, admitting his doubts whether he himself could beget a child. Here the paternal and erotic are embodied in separate characters. The aging husband and his ally, the father of the young man, are aligned against the young man, who has sailed off around the world after making love to the girl. The paternal faction triumphs. The young woman decides to stay with the husband who has provided a home for her child, even though she still loves the young man. When he returns, he is made to see the superiority of the older man's claim because of the services he has rendered.

The dual aspect of the father, as paternal and erotic, the daytime and the nighttime father, is a recurrent theme in French films. A major trend in adult fantasy seems to be an attempt to reassure the spectator that the erotic side is not as dangerous as it appears to children. This may be done by recognizing that the originally dissociated nighttime father is one with the daytime father, so that the paternal component may moderate the erotic. Or the nighttime aspect may turn out to be also benevolent, or it may be converted to benevolence. Or it may be shown to be only a false belief about a benevolent character. Where the dual character of the father remains most complete, the scene tends to be mythological or exotic. This reflects what we have supposed on other grounds to be a characteristic way of handling the dangerous sexual aspect of the father for French children: projecting it outside the house onto mythological creatures (*loup-garou, croquemitaine, ramponneau)* who may descend on children who do not close their eyes and go to sleep at night. An acknowledgment of this childhood source seems to appear in the remoteness or admittedly make-believe setting of certain films. The devil, who sends his emissaries to activate the erotic and jealous components of the good father in *Les Visiteurs du Soir,* is an illustration, although here there is also a tendency towards fusion in showing the dual potentialities of the good father. *L'Éternel Retour,* occurring in a timeless world of legend, presents two fathers, the ruffian who beats the heroine in the lowly place from which the hero rescues her, and the kindly uncle at home in the castle to whom she is brought back as a bride. Here too the good father figure in spite of himself presents a double aspect, as he prevents the happiness of the young couple. In the fairy tale, *La Belle et la Bête,* an inversion makes the beast an aspect of the son figure rather than of the father. The main development is the transformation of the beast from dangerous to tender and pathetic – his domestication.

The father in *Le Père Tranquille,* the setting of which is occupied France during the Second World War, leads a double life. Manifestly an aging man of declining powers, pottering around among the plants in his hothouse, he is secretly the leader of the local underground. More specifically, he presents different aspects to his wife and to his daughter.

His wife, who has lost any amorous appeal for him (he is mocking when she calls him "sweetheart" at bedtime), sees him only as a near-invalid whom she must bundle up warmly whenever he goes out. His daughter, more perceptive, picks up clues to his underground activities. One night when he is watching from an attic window for the explosion which will mark the accomplishment of a piece of sabotage which he has directed, the daughter joins him and watches admiringly the nocturnal fireworks for which she knows the father is responsible. The nighttime role of the father is here in the service of paternal motives, for the protection of the home (land).

In *Copie Conforme*, a harmless aging clerk who bears an exact likeness to an accomplished crook, is arrested on suspicion of having committed the other's crimes. A girl who works in the same office with him assures him that she is not taken in by his benevolent facade; she believes he is really someone quite different, and is intensely attracted by this imagined other side. The crook hires the clerk to double for him, to give him an alibi when he is out on a job. The crook's girl, who thus meets the clerk and supposes him to be the crook suddenly manifesting an unwonted gentleness, assures him happily: "I always knew you were a sentimentalist." Thus, each girl opposes the duality with the fantasy of one man who combines the two aspects. This is a joking reversal of the discovery that the originally-imagined two fathers are really one.

The more sombre *Panique* shows how a benevolent older man (who is ugly and who leads a mysterious solitary life) is wronged because people mistakenly attach to him the fantasy picture of the nighttime father. He is suspected of seducing little girls and murdering lone women. The beautiful girl with whom he falls in love is suspicious of his attentions, while he idealizes her and wants to protect her. So, far from being the love-monopolizing father, it is he who suffers disappointments: he sees through a window the woman he loves embracing a younger man – he has previously been deserted by his wife, who ran away with her lover.

As an aging man, the father figure is destined to become the outsider and onlooker, and thus he is forgiven for the disappointments which he imposed on the son in childhood. French films generally tend to make father figures sympathetic, by presenting them as themselves bearers of disappointment. The prominent father-daughter love theme focuses on the father at a moment when he in his turn is disappointed.

Though the father figure frequently fails to get what he wants, he usually controls the situation and can separate or unite the young couple. (*Panique* is an exception in this respect, as the older man is not only disappointed but also helpless.) In *Le Silence est d'Or*, the aging man complains that everyone wants him to play father. He has fallen in love with the daughter of an old sweetheart, having first assumed a guardian role towards her. The young man to whom he has been like a father also loves the girl, but is too loyal to enter into rivalry with him. The older man, a movie producer (in the early days of films), is directing the young couple in a scene in which the girl is a harem slave and the young man her lover. The prince to whom she belongs interrupts them and has the young man carried off by harem guards; the girl jumps out of the window. During the shooting of this scene the studio is being honored by the visit of an oriental potentate and his suite. The potentate does not like this ending and asks the producer to arrange a happier one. The actor playing the prince in the film then protests that it will make him look foolish if he gives up the girl. The producer persuades him, at the same time persuading himself to give up the girl in real life. In the revised ending of the film within the film, the young lovers are united. The two oriental princes, the one in the film and the one in the audience, express the two potentialities of the father – to separate or to unite the young couple.

As a counterpoint to the father's impulse to impede the love life of the son, he may act as the initiator of the young man. There is likely to be some irony in this as it leads to unforeseen rivalry. In *Le Silence est d'Or,* the older man consoles the younger one for having lost his girl, and demonstrates to him how to pick up a new girl. Later, the young man uses the technique thus acquired to strike up an acquaintance, unwittingly, with the girl whom the older man loves. In *L'Education du Prince,* an older man undertakes, at the suggestion of the young man's mother, to introduce the young men to a stylish kept woman. He does not discover until later that the woman is the mistress of his colleague, another aging man. Characteristically, the sexual longings of the older generation are aroused by the prospect of the initiation of the younger. The mother (a beautiful widowed queen of a mythical kingdom) seduces the man to whom she has confided the education of her son on the night when she supposes the son is having his first sexual experience. In *L'Eternel Retour,* by an inversion, the young man offers to find a bride for his aging uncle, and himself falls in love with the bride.

The rivalry of fathers and sons is thus amply acknowledged in French films, but it is mitigated in various ways. A major effort is made to transform the father from a threatening and overpowering figure to a sympathetic and even pitiable one. His feelings are understandable and he cannot be blamed for them. Without his intending or foreseeing it, his paternal feelings may shift to erotic ones. The spectator's awareness of this possibility makes the father all the more lovable when he resigns himself to the paternal. Because of his age, he usually suffers disappointment in his love for the younger woman, even where he succeeds in keeping the younger man from getting her. Resentment of this residue of his power is softened by the realization of his impotence and imminent death. In the relatively few cases where he gets the young woman it is after the young man has already been her lover *(Fanny, Sirocco)*. Frequently both father and son figures are disappointed, or must at least renounce some of their hopes. This sharing of disappointment, makes for a fellow feeling with the father on the part of the son. The father is forgiven and loved through the realization that even he (in French films, especially he) is not exempt from this disappointment.

There is in French films no comparable mitigation of the hostilities between mother and daughter figures. The deprivation that the older woman imposes on the younger tends to be more calculated; the disappointments which the older woman may suffer seem to provoke vindictive impulses towards the younger one. In *La Fille du Puisaiter,* the hero, who is suddenly called away for air force duty, asks his mother to go to a rendezvous and take his girl a note. The mother asks whether the girl is a *poule;* when he says she is a nice girl, she conceals her jealousy behind an irritated pretense that she is not interested. She goes to the rendezvous and when she sees the pretty young heroine approach, withdraws and tears up the note, leaving the girl to wait in vain. Later she casts doubt upon the likelihood that her son was responsible for the girl's pregnancy, pretending that she knows nothing about their relationship. In *L'Amour autour de la Maison,* an unattractive and embittered older sister is the guardian of a sweet and lovable younger sister. She wards off the younger sister's suitors, sometimes telling the girl that they are only interested in her money, sometimes telling the men that the girl is hopelessly ill. When the girl discovers that her sister has driven away the man she loves, she murders the sister and then goes mad. In the course of the film, the older sister has also tried to interfere with the happiness of another young girl whom she has seen with a boy friend. There is less rivalry for a disputed love object here than envy and the wish to deprive any woman who has what she lacks.

In *Étoile sans Lumière,* a film actress is in danger of losing her position through the introduction of sound films. She and her lover prevail on a naive young girl who has a remarkable singing voice to come to work for them. They take the girl away from her village and separate her from her boy friend; she lives at their house as a servant. When she sings at the studio, she does not understand that her voice will be dubbed in for the actress. When the film is shown, the actress is a greater success than ever before because of the singing. The girl, now feeling cheated, wants to get credit for her own voice and to become a star herself. The actress discourages her, meanly pointing out her lack of beauty, and assuring her that she could never succeed. When the actress is killed in an automobile accident, her lover tries to persuade the girl that her voice must die with the actress, so as not to detract from her memory. The girl nevertheless tries to give a concert. Haunted by the discouraging and forbidding image of the actress, she breaks down, is unable to sing, and is hooted from the stage. Mother figures thus have a destructive impact upon daughter figures. There is little of the counteracting restitutive tendency which we find in father figures, who frequently arrange the happiness of the young man whom they feel tempted to deprive.

While parents appear frequently and prominently, more often than not the parental couple is incomplete. The father-mother-son triangle tends to be replaced by that of father-daughter-son. There does not seem to be any trend to leave the widowed parent more often with the opposite than with the same sex child. Rather, the isolation of the child with the widowed parent seems to provide the possibility of concentrating with lucidity on this dyadic relation: father-son in *Marius,* father-daughter in *La Fille du Puisatier*, mother-daughter in *Macadam,* mother-son in *L'Education du Prince*. This fits in with the finding from other sources that there is a tendency in the French family to keep the relationship of any two members isolated from the others. This isolation of the dyadic relation would seem to be a defense against involvement in the Oedipal triangle. At the same time it may fulfil the wish to eliminate rivals.

Where both parents are present, we may find a child sharing a secret with one parent which they both keep from the other parent. Thus, in *Le Père Tranquille,* the daughter knows about the father's underground activities of which the mother remains unaware. In *La Fille du Puisatier,* the son tells only his mother about his love affair. She keeps it from his father.

In the relations of mothers and fathers to each other, one sometimes finds the father impotent and disintegrating, while the mother, still firm and active, assumes a dominant and somewhat contemptuous role. In *L'Eternel Retour,* the aging father is entirely preoccupied with his collection of swords and guns (a recurrent preoccupation of aging men in French films). His formidable wife impatiently recalls him to serious business, such as their problems about a prospective inheritance. The heroine's father in *La Passionnelle,* a retired officer, devotes himself to executing military maneuvers with an army of toy soldiers. His more realistically oriented wife demands that he pay some attention to arranging their daughter's marriage, which is necessary to save the family fortune. In *Le Père Tranquille,* the mother has an equally condescending, though somewhat kindlier attitude towards her husband, who seems only interested in his orchids, and whom she feels she must treat like a child. In this case, it is a false impression.

The recurrence of the grudging, embittered, disparaging, and vindictive mother figure suggests that the solution of the father-son conflict has been made at her expense. The substitution of a daughter figure as the main object of father-son rivalry leaves the aging woman without compensations. The attachment of a young man to an older woman, sometimes supposed to be frequent in life, does not seem to be reflected in these French films.

The Vicissitudes of Impulse

French films express conflicting feelings about the relation of human beings to nature. In *La Passionnelle,* when the heroine, the daughter of an old aristocratic family, protests against the marriage which her parents have arranged for her, her mother tells her that only animals marry for love. The mother's attitude is not presented very sympathetically, and the husband whom she is trying to force on her daughter for financial reasons is a stupid fop. However, the daughter's following of her impulses has led to more disastrous consequences than those which would presumably follow from this loveless marriage. She has had a love affair with a servant and, when he tries to blackmail her, she murders him.

In *Fanny,* the former lover of the heroine returns after a long absence to find her married to an older man, who has given his name to the child begotten by the lover. The lover urges his claims to the girl and is opposed by his own father, who takes the side of the elderly husband. When the young man argues that the child is his, the father retorts that animals procreate, and that there is more to being a father than that. The disputed woman, even though she loves the younger man, agrees that her husband is more a father to her child. He provided a bed with fine sheets for the child to be born in, let her dig her nails into his hand when she was giving birth, and supplied a large family of aunts and uncles who welcomed the child. As the forsaken offspring of the lover, it would not have been the same child.

When a child appears in French films, it is apt to be illegitimate or otherwise in danger of lacking a father. There seems to be the feeling that in procreation people have been carried away by irrational impulses. This is perhaps a wishful or warning fantasy of abandonment to impulse, as opposed to the careful family limitation presumably practised in life. Also there is the feeling, which we have already remarked upon, that there is a discontinuity between the function of the lover in begetting the child and that of the father in protecting and caring for it (cf. *Fanny* and *La Fille du Puisatier*). In *Sirocco,* when the heroine's lover disappears, leaving her pregnant, she meets an older man who falls in love with her, marries her, and accepts her child as his own. In *Les Enfants du Paradis,* the hero's little son is in danger of losing his father, because of the hero's great love for a more alluring woman than his wife. Here it is the presence of two types of women (corresponding to the two types – or two tendencies – of men) that threatens the security of the child. In *Vertiges,* the hero's son is in danger of losing his father, who is suffering from a serious brain disease. Thus, where children appear, there is a tendency to suggest that uncontrollable natural forces both produce and threaten them.

In *Farrebique,* an attempt is made photographically to assimilate the birth of a child to the order of nature, with unintended contradictory effects. The pregnancy of the farmer's wife is associated with a long series of images of opening flowers and the activities of domestic and woodland animals. The length of the sequence produces an effect of protesting too much. An explanatory voice accompanies the pictures, intellectualizing the more dreamlike appeal of the visual images. (A sequence on winter, not associated with procreation, did not require the verbal accompaniment.) The pictures of flowers opening are produced by stop-camera photography, altering the natural tempo of growth. Thus, a human design is superimposed on nature, just as when the French clip trees into symmetrical shapes. The farmers in the film are never shown either as responding to, or as identifying themselves with the processes of natural growth as pictorially presented. The association with beasts and flowers is a poetic conceit of the sophisticated film producer.

L'Education du Prince presents the reconciliation of the natural and the artificial in farcical terms. A prince, exiled from a mythical kingdom, who is being groomed to return to his throne, is in love with a bargekeeper's daughter. He prevails upon his mentor, a teacher of manners, to go with him on an excursion in the country with the girl, her father, and a crowd of young people. The teacher is impressed with the novel experience of getting up at dawn and going fishing with the bargekeeper. This contact with nature persuades him to consent to the marriage of the prince to the girl he loves. However, this will not involve any abrogation of aristocratic procedure. Rather, he provides the girl with bogus patents of nobility and makes the bargekeeper an admiral in the mythical kingdom navy.

Contacts between members of different social strata may be beneficial or dangerous. In *Panique,* a man of upper-class origin loses his life through involvement with a girl he meets in a lower-class quarter. In *Quai des Orfèvres,* a marriage to a lower-class girl is nearly fatal for a man of good family. Such films recall Zola's preoccupation with the damaging effects of contact between the higher and lower orders. In *La Passionnelle,* the direction is reversed; an idealistic lower-class youth is destroyed through his love for a bad girl of superior station. By contrast, *La Fille du Puisatier* shows a wealthy middle-class family being transformed in the direction of warmer human feelings by contact with a family of lower status. In *Circonstances Atténuantes,* the contact between superior and inferior is mutually beneficial, as a gang of thieves teach an aging prosecutor and his wife to enjoy life once more, while he converts them to going straight. Thus, there is an effort to believe that it is safe and even beneficial to disregard conventional boundaries; at the same time there are recurrent doubts about this.

French films emphasize the dangers of two major forms of emotion: the tenacity of attachment to an unworthy or otherwise disappointing person, and, as already mentioned, the tendency for protective paternal feelings to change unexpectedly into sexual longings. A man may commit himself irretrievably to a beautiful woman, so that nothing he learns about her can alter his feelings (*La Passionnelle, Quai des Orfèvres, Les Enfants du Paradis*). Similarly, a woman may remain bound to a man who is a criminal (she sacrifices herself and others to help cover up his crimes, in *Panique),* or who treats her cruelly (she commits suicide after a final rebuff, in *Falbalas).* Cases in which paternal feelings towards a young woman change into amorous ones have already been discussed.

In French films, impulses are subject to a variety of transformations, and may shift from one form of expression to another. Different modes of expression may be mutually antagonistic. Two major alternatives are preoccupations with property and with love. A life oriented to property, with monotonous petty hostilities, may be disrupted by the break-through of love, with its more dramatic potentialities for happiness or tragedy. *Goupi-Mains Rouges* begins with a provincial family whose interests are concentrated on property. The great-grandfather keeps the secret of where a treasure in gold is concealed, and everyone is afraid he will die before he tells where it is. The relations among the various members of the extensive household are carping, grudging, and spiteful, but also stable and nonclimactic. To insure the continuation of the family, the great-grandson has been called home from Paris to marry his cousin. On the night of his arrival, a series of half-comical, half-sinister events dramatize the young man's recollection of frightening childhood fantasies, connected both with his return home and his imminent marriage, and at the same time express the typical participation of the whole family in the sexual initiation of the young. The young man is terrified by his uncle, who tells him lurid stories on the way home from the station, and by a young male cousin, who appears in a bizarre costume to chase him away (a revival of the nighttime bogey). The same night, an old aunt is murdered in the woods. The great-grandfather drinks too much and has a stroke; the young man, entering the house, finds him stretched out, apparently dead, on the floor. He runs away and spends the night in the woods. Next day, when the aunt's murder is being investigated, he is asked whether he did not see or hear anything during the night; he insists that he was asleep (the defense of the child in connection with nighttime observations). Despite these major disturbances that herald the irruption of love into a property-oriented existence, the relation of the young couple develops favorably, and, in the end, the transmission of the property is insured by the communication of the great-grandfather's secret. The disrupting episode of mating is successfully assimilated into the monotonous continuity of property transmission.

In *L'Éternel Retour,* the shift from property to love has tragic effects. In the beginning, a rich and aging widower is surrounded by his prospective heirs, whose relations are disagreeable. A young nephew undertakes to find a bride for the older man, then falls in love with her himself. A fatal love rivalry replaces the petty antagonisms of the rival heirs.

Characters in French films may content themselves with attentuated satisfactions, but subsequently recover full impulsive vigor. *Circonstances Atténuantes* shows an aging couple who have resigned themselves to a hypochondriacal decline. They restrict themselves to an ascetic diet and visit health resorts where they drink purgative waters. On the way to such a resort, their car breaks down, and they are forced to spend the night at an inn frequented by a gang of thieves. They are served spiced dishes and wine, and, fearful of offending their rough-looking hosts, they eat and drink. Far from suffering the anticipated ill effects, they find themselves feeling much better. Stimulated by the food and drink, the wife dances with one of the gangsters and the husband starts flirting with a pretty girl. With these combined facilitations, the aging couple are able to recapture long suspended sexual pleasures.

The central character in *Panique* exhibits a variety of impulse transformations. In the neighborhood where he lives, he carries on a hobby of constantly snapping candid-camera shots. In another part of the city, under a different name, he maintains an office where he gives confidential advice to people who come and confide their troubles and secrets. Thus, he is absorbed in voyeuristic activities on two levels, which are kept distinct by his double life. We later learn that he once had a wife whom he deeply loved, who ran away with another man. After this disappointment, he abandoned his upper-class home and voluntarily sank to humble surroundings and to his lonely absorption in his looking hobbies. His looking takes a more direct form as he becomes interested in a beautiful woman who lives across the way, and whom he watches nightly through the window. As he becomes acquainted with her, he feels love for the first time in years, and begins to revert to the level of his former existence, symbolized by his return to his long abandoned mansion.

A recurrent theme is that of the old man with a gun. In his decline, he manifests an exclusive attachment to substitute symbols of masculinity. An old man in *La Femme du Boulanger,* who is mocked by the cuckolded baker with the remark, "You couldn't even be a cuckold!" perpetually carries a gun. The grandfather in *Goupi-Mains Rouges* practises sharpshooting around the house. The aging man in *L'Eternel Retour* devotes himself to polishing and cleaning his large collection of guns and swords.

Sexual needs are apt to be present in every character in French films. They are not confined to the central characters, but are equally operative in their friends, relatives, chauffeurs, and grocery clerks. They are not confined to handsome young people, but are also active in fathers, grandfathers, widowed mothers, and bespectacled little girls. This omnipresence of sexual impulses is expressed in the wealth of eccentricities in French film characters, for where the individual cannot find usual modes of gratification for such impulses, other forms are substituted. Characters who express these impulses in eccentric ways are presented sympathetically to the audience, but for the other characters in the film they are presented as the object of deep suspicion, even of persecution. The hero of *La Passionnelle* is a noble character, generous and protective of the weak, but he leads a solitary life, shunning the convivial pursuits appropriate to a young man. His main private occupation is peeping at a beautiful young girl through a window across from his own. His fellow townsmen despise and mock him, and eventually falsely suspect him of murder. The eccentric hero of *Panique,* with his similar isolation and voyeuristic hobbies, is subject to a like suspicion.

The Accidents of Justice

In French films the relation between crime and punishmeent is variable. The guilty may go unpunished, the falsely suspect may succumb. There is little confidence on the part of the innocent that they will be able to clear themselves; once suspected by the police, they feel like committing suicide. On the other hand, ironically, the guilty may be unable, despite their efforts, to gain credence for their confessions. The perpetrator of a perfect crime may die suffering from the frustration that no one will ever give him credit for what he has done.

In *Non Coupable*, the hero, who is otherwise a failure, discovers that he has an exceptional talent for crime. He murders his mistress' lover in such a way that the mistress is implicated, and then engineers the death of the mistress so that it appears to be an accident. His pride at having committed these perfect crimes impels him to confess, to gain acknowledgment for his genius. The authorities, however, interpret his confession as a touching effort to clear his mistress' name, and he is helplessly unable to transform his reputation for being a good-natured incompetent. In the end he writes a detailed account of the crimes and shoots himself. His cat, frightened by the shot, jumps onto the mantel where the confession is propped up in front of the clock, and the confession falls into the fire and burns.

The complaint which seems to be made against the authorities in French films is that they are too casual in reading men's souls. They accept what appears on the surface and do not probe into the depths. A French hero is less anxious to be cleared than he is to be understood. Thus, there is an equal irony in being falsely accused and mistakenly exonerated. In *La Passionnelle,* the heroine, a beautiful, pure-looking young girl, fails to get anyone to believe that she has murdered her lover. The gloomy, solitary young hero who has always been misunderstood, allows himself to be arrested for her crime. Where the murderer is known in French films, he is apt to be known to someone not in authority, who is unable to make the truth prevail over the false account with which the authorities are satisfied.

In *Panique,* an innocent man dies because he is falsely suspected of murder. Suspicion falls on him largely because no one recognizes the noble character which he conceals behind an eccentric facade. In the end, pursued by the police and an excited mob, he flees over a roof, slips, hangs by his hands from the gutter, and falls just as the police ladder is about to reach him. A few minutes after his death, a police inspector discovers the evidence by which the real murderer is identified.

This missing by a narrow margin is a recurrent theme. In respect to justice, there is the suggestion that, if the truth is discovered, it is still a matter of chance whether the discovery will be made before it is too late. In *Quai des Orfèvres,* the falsely suspected man is saved by a lucky coincidence. Imprisoned and hopeless of clearing himself, he cuts his wrists; the prisoner in the next cell happens to see the trickle of blood and raises an alarm in time for him to be revived. At the same time, the police inspector on the case turns up a clue linking another man to the crime. The police inspector here is a highly idiosyncratic character with an exceptional sympathy for human weaknesses. Nevertheless, he is ready to slap the falsely suspected man around to make him confess. Despite his weary conscientiousness about his work it does not seem that he would have discovered the real murderer if the man had not, by chance, been brought in on another charge.

In *Copie Conforme,* there is another demonstration of the tendency of the authorities to persist in their confusions. Two men who look exactly alike, one a clerk and the other a confidence man, end with reversed identities. The clerk first is arrested and charged with the other's crimes, but is allowed to go free after an inconclusive investigation. When he is about to commit suicide because his reputation has been tarnished, the crook offers him the job of providing him with alibis. When, after an involved life together the confidence man dies violently, the authorities insist on confusing their identities. The dead man bears the name of the clerk and is credited with having concealed an amazing career of crime behind a harmless facade, while the real clerk survives with another man's identity and possessions, including an attractive girl friend.

Such films express in part the difficulty of disentangling good from evil. It seems to be taken for granted that everyone has capacities for wickedness as well as goodness. A film like *Copie Conforme* mocks the attempt to isolate good and bad characters. In *Quai des Orfèvres,* a man and his wife, both moderately sympathetic characters, each might have killed a man who, as it happened, was murdered by a third person.

The agencies pursuing a criminal investigation also display an admixture of baser motives. In *Panique,* the excited mob which closes in on the innocent hero is interspersed with *gendarmes* who do nothing to restrain the assault. In *Le Corbeau,* a mob of townspeople, enraged by a series of anonymous letters, take the pursuit of the criminal out of the hands of the ineffectual authorities and almost lynch an innocent woman.

Circonstances Atténuantes expresses in comedy form the intimate connection which may exist between the prosecution and the enactment of crime. The hero, an aging retired prosecutor, finds himself vacationing by chance in a den of thieves. When their company turns out to have a surprisingly rejuvenating effect, he in return instructs them about which crimes involve the least risk of punishment. Soon he plays the role of leader of the gang, and hugely enjoys plotting a robbery, even though it is his own house that is robbed (they remove the knick-knacks with which his wife had encumbered it and to which he had always objected), and even though his rather indirectly achieved aim is to reform the gang.

The one who is falsely suspected, as already noted, tends not to put up a struggle against false charges. On the contrary, he is likely to attempt suicide *(Quai des Orfèvres, Copie Conforme),* or to submit himself to undeserved punishment (*La Passionnelle*). The falsely accused, as we have seen, usually has an acknowledged motive for the crime of which he is suspected, but he has not been able to carry the motive into action. Nevertheless, once the act has been committed, he behaves as if he were guilty of it. The mistaken accusations of the authorities thus have a double irony. The authorities are mistaken in their reconstruction of the facts; at the same time they do not know how right they are from the point of view of the hero's bad conscience and his need for punishment. Similarly, when the authorities mistakenly exonerate the guilty, they do not know how well they punish them, by frustrating their need for punishment. The hero of *Non Coupable* is forced to be his own executioner. The general tone of not blaming anyone, which pervades French films, seems to be related to this readiness to acknowledge one's own bad impulses.

Women murderers are usually presented sympathetically. Violence which men are unable to express directly may be embodied in a sympathetic woman. (Marianne and Joan of Arc remain the symbols of embattled France.) In *Le Corbeau,* it is a woman who in the end kills the author of a poison pen campaign by which the whole town has been terrorized. In *La Passionnelle,* the heroine murders her lover and the hero takes the blame. The hero had hated the victim long before he knew of his relation to the heroine. The victim had been a coarse and popular man, who had mocked the dreamy, solitary hero, and once the hero had knocked him down to protect a poor matchgirl from his unwanted attentions. Yet, it was the heroine who committed the murder.

The theme of the woman defending herself replaces that of the man defending her. Nevertheless, making the woman the agent does not give the man a clear conscience. The hero accepts the blame for the action which was his in intent, under the guise of protecting the woman from punishment. The suicidally inclined false suspect in *Quai des Orfèvres* is similarly motivated; he had intended to commit the murder and he suspects that his wife has done it. *Non Coupable* presents this pattern in reverse. The hero makes his mistress appear to be guilty of his crimes, and then unsuccessfully attempts to take the blame himself.

The high suicide rate of characters in French films is further evidence of the degree of interference with direct expressions of aggression. Suicide is the most likely recourse of both men and women who are driven to violence by frustration in love. In *Sirocco,* the hero, whose wife had disappeared – supposing him dead – carries on an unwearying quest for her, finally finds her married to another man and shoots himself. His suicide is preceded by ineffectual destructive gestures towards both his wife and his successor. He invites the wife, who still loves him, to meet him in a low hotel room, and brings in a crowd of his comrades to whom he exposes her as a prostitute. He visits the second husband, waves a gun at him, makes a high-flown speech, and withdraws. Love suicides tend to be associated with such ineffectual gestures of attack against the rival or the disappointing loved one. In *Falbalas,* the hero jumps from a window clasping in his arms a dress dummy in a bridal gown; to his hallucinated vision the dummy appears to be the girl he loves. In *Le Revenant,* the young man who has been dismissed by his dancer sweetheart, throws himself down from the overhead catwalk onto the stage where she is dancing. He does not hit anyone, and the fall turns out not to be fatal to him either. The ineffectiveness of the suicide's last aggressive gesture seems to show that the unhappy individual's victim can only be himself. The other whom he tries to drag down with him is only a fantasy figure, a dummy.

Acknowledgment of the reality of death is prominent in French films. This is evidenced by the fairly frequent introduction of funerals. Even when a funeral is joked about, its significance is confirmed rather than denied.

In *Circonstances Atténuantes* a funeral procession appears quite unrelated to the plot, but emotionally congruent as a *memento mori.* As an aging woman stands on a balcony in the embrace of a newly acquired young lover, a funeral procession passes opposite. The young man tips his cap without interrupting the kiss. In *Farrebique,* the funeral of the grandfather culminates the protracted tracing of his decline and reluctant transfer of the family property to his son. In *L'Amour Autour de la Maison,* a highborn woman falls in love, for the first time in her life, with a rather wild-looking recluse. After some hesitation, she arranges a rendezvous with him, but she waits for him in vain; he has been killed in a shooting accident. In a despair which she cannot show, she sees his body carried home, and later watches the simple funeral march.

Other films evoke a painful awareness of the imminence of death. In *Jéricho,* a group of hostages, during the occupation, spend the night in a church awaiting execution at dawn. The collaborationist among them mounts the pulpit and delivers a sermon: "Let us try to purchase life at any price. If we die, a monument in our honor will in due course be unveiled one sunny afternoon on the main square of the town. Who will drink the beer, flirt with the girls, walk in the sun that afternoon? Not we, We will have ceased to be. What will it matter to us ?" The hostages are at the last moment rescued by an Allied air attack. This ending does not, however, cancel the impression of facing unavoidable death. The characters have been helplessly awaiting their death, which the last minute rescue only postpones. In *Vertiges,* the hero, a physician, becomes aware that he is suffering from an almost certainly fatal disease. He takes an x-ray photograph of his brain and discovers a tumor (a pictorial transcription of the Existentialist saying that if man examines himself he discovers he is going to die). He devotes what he believes will be his last months to alienating his wife, so that she will suffer less from losing him, and to earning as much money as possible, so as to leave his family well provided for. In the commercial laboratory job which he takes, he succeeds in making a great discovery, and is just receiving the congratulations of his staff when he collapses. While it turns out not to be too late for the hero to be saved by an operation, the impression of imminent death remains.

The readiness to acknowledge the reality of death in French films is perhaps in part related to the French acknowledgment of one's own bad impulses, which is expressed also in the weakness of the struggle of the falsely accused. In part, the acknowledgment of death seems related to a pervasive tendency to inure oneself to the disappointing aspects of life by facing them.

Varieties of Disappointment

French films frequently re-evoke the disappointment of childhood situations of being an onlooker. The hero first secretly watches a beautiful woman, idealizes her, and falls in love with her. Later he has the disillusioning experience of seeing her together with another man. Since, despite this disillusionment, he may be unable to detach his feelings from her, the outcome is apt to be a tragic one for him. In *Panique,* the hero, watching a beautiful young woman through a window across the way, eventually sees her joined by her lover. In *La Passionnelle,* when the hero finally enters the beautiful young girl's bedroom, into which he had so often peeped from across the way, it is to find the body of her murdered lover on the bed. In each case the hero remains attached to the woman, and is sacrificed by her in order to cover up a crime of violence in which she and her lover are involved. In *La Passionnelle,* the woman has defended herself by murdering the attacking man, and makes the hero her accomplice in asking him to help her conceal the crime. The emphasis on the woman defending herself, and on the enforcement of a guilty secrecy for her sake on the part of the onlooker seems to be a specifically French nuance.

The pattern is subject to a number of variations. In *Panique,* the woman deceives the hero into believing that she needs to be protected from her lover. However, the lover, she knows, has murdered a woman. The hero secretly knows it too, but delays revealing his knowledge. At the same time, without his realizing it, the woman and her lover are using him to cover up the crime by pinning it on him; he dies as a result of this.

The dramatic re-creation of a disappointment is a way of turning passivity into activity: one now makes the thing happen which one had originally suffered involuntarily. This is emphasized in films where the hero directs a play within a play reproducing his own disappointment. In *Les Enfants du Paradis,* the hero has hesitated to make love on short acquaintance to the beautiful woman whom he adores; she becomes the mistress of his friend. He composes a pantomime in which the three appear. The woman is a goddess on a pedestal; he is a sad clown who only looks at her and worships her; when he falls asleep at the foot of the pedestal, the lover appears, and she descends to embrace him. In *Le Silence est d'Or,* the hero directs a film in which the girl he loves is separated from his successful rival; he then revises the ending to express his renunciation of the girl. In the end he watches the completed film, which shows the happy union of the young couple. The hero's revision of his film typifies the preference in French films generally for facing a disappointment rather than denying it.

Le Revenant presents a variation on the theme of dramatic reproduction of one's own disappointment. The hero returns to the town where he had once suffered a serious disappointment in love. Now a successful ballet impresario, he introduces his premiere ballerina to the nephew of the woman he formerly loved. The ballerina leads the young man on, then reveals to him that she has a lover. The hero has the satisfaction of seeing another undergo, as a result of his manipulation, a repetition of his disappointment. In the end, the older and younger man go away together. We may recall here that in resolving rivalry and hostility between father and son, the recognition that they both suffer disappointment is a major factor.

In *Falbalas,* the attempt to handle artistically the relation of the woman to another man breaks down; its aim is to deny rather than to face disappointment. The hero, a successful *couturier,* conceals from himself the significance of his occupation as a means of exhibiting the woman to another man, her future husband (as expressed in the traditional conclusion of a Paris opening by the display of a wedding gown). He regards the gowns as his own creations, the means of his own exhibition, and reduces the woman to a mere mannequin. His relations with women otherwise show a strong defense against any serious involvement. When he meets the fiancée of his friend, and undertakes to design a trousseau for her, he unexpectedly falls in love for the first time, His preoccupation with his own exhibition gives way to the revived image of the happy couple from which he is excluded. In the end he commits suicide.

The inability of the man to detach himself from the disappointing woman suggests that her relation to the other man, though always manifestly a source of suffering, is also gratifying. Where a bad woman appears in opposition to a good woman, the bad woman is almost invariably preferred *(Torrents, Macadam, Quai des Orfèvres, Les Enfants* du *Paradis, Copie Conforme, Fric-Frac).* A characteristic treatment of the bad woman shows her etherealized, detached and superior to the life she leads, or invested with a metaphysical significance. Thus, a prostitute may appear as a beautiful supernatural creature, and her procurer as the devil, who sends her to tempt and destroy *(Les Visiteurs du Soir).* In *Les Enfants du Paradis,* a beautiful promiscuous woman appears to be somehow untouched by anything that happens to her. She is the same whether she is exhibiting herself naked in the side show of a fair or living in sheltered luxury as the wife of a nobleman. She has only one great love, for the hero, which, however, does not divert her life course. The sensitive hero remains intensely bound to her, reacting as it seems to an essence which is distinct from the accidents of her life. Beside her, the devoted good girl, whom he marries, is uninteresting. In addition to seeing the bad woman in an ideal light, French films also present the bad woman who becomes transformed through love (the prostitutes in *Sirocco* and *Macadam).*

Contact with another man achieved through the disappointing woman appears in *La Passionnelle.* The hero has had an intense, hostile relation with another man who is his opposite, convivial and lusty where he is shy and ascetic. After he has discovered this man as the murdered lover of the heroine, he carries his body through the town late at night. Stopped by a passerby, he props up the body in his arms, explains that they are returning from a drinking bout. Thus in grim pretense, he becomes a companion of the other man. Less somberly in *Le Revenant,* the two disappointed men go away together. In *Falbalas,* as we have noted, the condition of the hero's falling in love is the association of the woman with a man who is his close friend.

The acknowledgment of the man's disappointment with the woman seems to function in these films in a variety of ways. The acknowledgment helps to work through the residues of past disappointments and to arm the characters against the impact of their probable recurrence. Attempts at denial are likely to lead to disaster; a disillusioned clarity of vision guards against being taken by surprise. The recognition of common experiences of disappointment is presented as a major factor in mitigating rivalry between fathers and sons. The infidelity of the beloved woman has a rewarding aspect, which makes it impossible to give her up, or to prefer a good woman to her, in that she mediates between her two men.

Where a woman is the disappointed onlooker (a situation less frequently and less elaborately developed), the emphasis seems to be more on her envy of the other woman than on jealousy of the man. In *L'Amour Autour de la Maison,* an embittered woman looks on, through the window of a summer house, at the love-making of a pretty young girl and her sweetheart. The woman, who has never had a lover, had previously arranged a rendezvous with the man she loved in the same summer house, but he was accidentally killed before he was to come. She is not a rival for the love of the young man whom she sees with the girl; she is only envious of the girl. In *Le Corbeau,* a precocious, homely little girl weeps in frustrated rage after having spied her aunt's lover entering the aunt's bedroom. Even when the man who is spied on is loved by the onlooking woman, the experience has a preponderant note of envy of the other woman for the qualities which give her the advantage. The aging wife in *Symphonie Pastorale* watches through the window an affectionate scene between her husband and their young and beautiful adopted daughter.

Another major occasion for disappointment is a discrepancy in timing, a discrepancy between wish and opportunity. The opportunity may occur before the emotional readiness to seize it; when the emotional readiness is there, the opportunity is there no longer. Or the reverse may occur: a satisfaction is granted when the wish for it is no longer felt. In the *Marius-Fanny* series, the young man leaves the girl who loves him, to go away to sea. By the time he realizes how intensely he wants her, she is already married to another man. In *Falbalas,* the girl with whom the hero is only playing offers to break her engagement for his sake. He alienates her by telling her he is not serious. Later, when he discovers that he is in love with her, she is no longer interested. In *Les Enfants du Paradis,* the hero already loves the heroine when he renounces the opportunity to make love to her; they hardly know each other, and he has too much delicacy and awe of her. Through a series of intervening accidents, it is years before the opportunity recurs. They try to pretend that they have their chance again on the same terms, but their attempt at self-deception is not successful. Too many things have changed; he has married and has a child. After one night together, the woman leaves presumably never to return.

In *Sirocco,* the hero falls in love with a prostitute whom he sees in an idealized light. She becomes transformed through her love for him. They are separated and, believing him dead, she marries another man. When the hero finally finds her again, he calls her a whore. He does not understand that she loves only him, and has married only to give a home to his child. Thus, while the woman has become transformed in one direction, the man's fantasy of her has changed in the opposite direction. At both ends there is a discrepancy between fantasy and reality.

In *Le Revenant,* the more usual order is reversed. The woman whom in youth the hero loved is in middle age ready to desert her bourgeois marriage for his sake, but he no longer wants her. The boon once so wished for is granted too late. In *Le Silence est d'Or,* the hero's film studio is honored by the visit of an oriental potentate and his suite. He and his whole staff are decorated with medals. Preoccupied with his unhappy love for his young star, he is unable to enjoy this success. In *Falbalas,* the hero's new dress collection is receiving enthusiastic applause as, disoriented by his disappointment in love, he walks uncomprehendingly through the show room.

A possible source of this tragedy of timing may be found in the parent-child relation. There is some evidence to suggest that French mothers are extremely indulgent and caressing to young infants, for instance, talking to them continuously and lovingly before they can understand a word. Presumably later, when the child becomes more demanding, the mother becomes less gratifying. Thus, there may be an impression that what is now so longed for and unattainable was once offered when one did not sufficiently appreciate it. A second reversal may occur for the adolescent boy, whose mother may want to cling to him when he is trying to free himself from her. The love so hopelessly sought in the earlier period may now seem more available and less wanted.

Another, closely related mode of disappointment is to miss by a narrow margin. In *L'Eternel Retour,* the hero dies just a moment before the woman he loves reaches him. In *Panique,* the hero falls from the roof just a moment before the police ladder reaches him. In *Clandestine,* the Nazis put out the Jewish doctor's eyes just a moment before his comrades rescue him. The doctor has sacrificed his eyes to keep a secret from men who are killed before they could have made any use of it. In *Farrebique,* the old father is about to realize his long-cherished dream of rebuilding the house. The son whose help he needs breaks a leg and the work must be postponed for the next year, which the father does not live to see.

A chain of repeated disappointments may extend from one generation to another. In *Torrents,* the hero's mother and the father of his fiancée had suffered from an unhappy love; each had married someone else, the woman had died and the man was left to mourn her. In the younger generation, the engagement is broken off; while still loving each other, each marries someone else, the woman commits suicide, and the hero is last seen standing mournfully beside the waterfall into which she had plunged.

Crowds in French films are frequently used to express the unreliability, obstructiveness, and incomprehension of the world. In *Non Coupable,* the hero stands with a friend looking out of a window at the faces of a crowd, who have gathered in front of a newspaper office awaiting news about a sensational murder. The hero points out one or another member of the crowd, and suggests that each might have committed the murder. As the hero is himself the murderer, it seems that the imputation of destructiveness to the crowd is a projection of one's own impulses. The lynching mobs in *Le Corbeau* and *Panique* have already been mentioned. If the attack of the crowd represents the projected destructiveness of their victim, then a certain justice is concealed behind the apparent misdirection of the attack. Similarly, as we remarked, the false accusation which cannot be resisted because of the character's bad wishes, shows that the authorities are right in a sense they do not understand.

In the final scene of *Les Enfants du Paradis,* the heroine disappears into the crowd, and the hero, desperately pursuing her, is obstructed by the dense mass of people moving in the opposite direction. Since the relation between the hero and heroine is illicit and threatens his family, the uncomprehending crowd functions as an embodiment of convention opposing the fulfillment of desire.

The applause of the crowd tends to be awarded at the wrong time or to the wrong person. We have already mentioned the applause of the audiences in *Falbalas* and *Le Silence est d'Or,* which comes at a time when the hero is unable to enjoy it. In *Le Revenant,* by the time the hero, a ballet impresario, wins the applause of the crowd, he is too embittered by the disappointments of his lonely and impoverished youth to feel much pleasure in it. When the hero in *Quai des Orfèvres* has made his wife a success as a singer, he is too distracted by jealousy to enjoy the applause she wins. The sense of the crowd as alien and unwittingly mocking in their discrepancy of mood is further expressed when the hero waits at the back of a gay audience in a variety theatre before going to murder the man he suspects of being his wife's lover. In *Étoile sans Lumière,* the audience's applause is awarded to the wrong person. The screen star gets an ovation for the singing of another woman which has been dubbed in. When the singer herself tries to make a stage appearance, she breaks down and is hooted by the audience.

French films may be compared with two contrasting types of drama. In one, we see the just triumph of the hero, based on the denial and projection of forbidden wishes. This is the major pattern of American films. In the other, we see the just death of the hero, following from the explicit or implicit acknowledgment of forbidden wishes, the pattern of classical and Shakespearean tragedy. Both of these dramatic types, while differing from each other, revolve around moral issues. In contrast to both, French films emphasize the acknowledgment of reality rather than the fantasy of an unreal moral order. They show repeatedly that deprivations and rewards may be equally undeserved. The events of real life do not coincide with justice. There is no supernatural justice, and human authorities are incompetent either to find out the facts or to understand men's souls. Nor is the world arranged to satisfy human wishes. Something happening a moment sooner or a moment later may make all the difference between our happiness and ruin; but this is mere chance. The reiteration of these not easily acceptable facts may help to reduce disappointment by not expecting too much. A little, fragile, brief pleasure is possible in life, though by no means assured; but man will only jeopardize it if he demands the impossible. Underneath this acceptance of disappointment, and facilitating it, there may be, as we have suggested, unadmitted feelings of guilt. However, they do not give rise to the tragedy of moral punishment. Life in its very nature punishes sufficiently.

VI. AN ANALYSIS OF FRENCH PROJECTIVE TESTS

Projective testing, particularly by means of inkblots and pictures, is one of the techniques that is being employed extensively in the study of cultures.[1] In Research in Contemporary Cultures some limited use has been made of projective materials, particularly among Chinese[2] and French informants.[3]

What we looked for mostly in the French projective materials were recurrent themes in the protocol content and for ways in which the material was approached, perhaps ways that could be called mechanisms of defense or positive and negative attitudes toward the blot, picture, or drawing situation. We searched for consistency and outstanding characteristics in the responses to the tests in much the same way one would look for recurrent themes and plots in films or literature – which we were, in fact, doing concurrently with French material. We then attempted to connect up these content themes and modes of response to other sorts of information we were obtaining about French culture. Sometimes we worked the other way around, getting a suggestion from informant interviews and seeing whether this idea was in any way reflected in the projective material.

Attitudes Toward the Tests

Our French informants were apologetic about the responses they gave to the stimulus material. They were willing to co-operate, but with the understanding that they were not to be considered typically French and that from them we would never learn about French culture. One informant said that from her we would learn nothing about France, that we could readily see that she was "sorcière et stupide, aussi un peu pixolée" (a witch and stupid, also a little addlepated). Another subject made excuses for having no imagination, a characteristic she considered individual and not French. This attitude was expressed not only in the testing situations but occurred again and again in informant interviews; an attitude which essentially stood for "from me you will not learn about the French but I am glad to do what I can for you," or, "my life was different from others, I am not representative." This attitude is the more striking in that it did not occur among Chinese informants either in interviews or in test situations; rather the Chinese felt more representative of China and did not resist such identification. This resistance on the part of the French informants of accepting stereotyping and their feeling of being unique and idiosyncratic may be tied up with their whole approach to life in which individuality is stressed, with at the same time a strong feeling for their own *civilisation*. Perhaps when visiting or living in a foreign land they feel the burden of transmitting French *civilisation* to the world around them an oppressive affair. This orientation toward being French, with conscious exclusion of what is "strange" ("strange" both within themselves and in their surroundings) and hence not French, may be accentuated in French people living not at home, in their *foyers* around which French life is so highly focused.

The Bogey

Our informants repeatedly confirmed in interviews that children are threatened with vague dark creatures, always male, the *loup-garou, croque-mitaine, ramponneau,* and so on (in North Africa he is sometimes referred to as an *arabe),* who may carry them off in a sack, rape them, and possibly eat them. This bogey figure was interpreted by us as a split-father image of the dangerous aspect of the father, which gets displaced into a vague region outside the home. This split of the father was also found to recur in films (e. g., *Les Visiteurs du* Soir, *L'Éternel Retour, La Belle et la Belle, Panique,* etc.). From informants we learned that croque-mitaine was dressed in black and that he carried a black sack. Two informants (mother and daughter) reported that the *croque-mitaine* is a creature of the night and that he is invoked specifically when the child does not want to go to sleep. The child is frightened by things he does not understand. The daughter informant remarked about the *loup-garou*, "C'est imprécis pour moi, c'est vague" (It is not precise for me, not clear). Thus we may see in the parents' invocation of the nighttime bogey a threat against the child's nocturnal curiosity. He must close his eyes and not inquire further. If he keeps his eyes open, the *loup-garou* will pop a sack over his head. One of our male informants said that his mother would threaten him if he did not go to sleep at night sometimes by having his father come upstairs; at other times the threat was of the *croque-mitaine*. According to our hypothesis, the vague, indefinite, nighttime dangerous male creature could be the father in his nighttime role. But instead of the father as threatener of the child, there is usually substituted the mythological bogey. This has a possible double effect of reducing the dangerousness of the real father and making his dangerous double a fictitious creature in whom the child soon ceases to believe.

On the Rorschach blots our subjects responded with remarkable regularity to re-evocation of monsters, usually mythological and creatures of the night, vague, dark and threatening. Card IV (regarded by some Rorschach workers as particularly evocative of the father image) elicited the largest number of direct references to a menacing dark monster. One woman informant called Card IV "un monstre" (a monster). She then elaborated in the inquiry by saying: "Avez-vous entendu l'histoire de l'arbre qui se remuait et qui est un monstre, énorme, terrible, prêt d'attaquer quelqu'un, lourd et horrible, marchant pesamment?" (Have you heard the story of the tree that moved and which is a monster, enormous, terrible, ready to attack someone, heavy, and horrible, walking ponderously ?) A young man called this blot "un espèce de monstre de caverne. Yeux d'homard. Oiseau de proie, de ruine" (a sort of monster of the cave. Eyes of a lobster, bird of prey, of ruin), and as another response to the same card he adds: "la tête brouillée, ni homme ni bête, plongée dans une espèce de nuit inquiète et inhumaine" (the head confused, neither man nor beast, plunged into a kind of night, restless and inhuman). This subject responds to Card V in similar but yet more vivid manner, "Impressionant. La belle et la bête. Une crinière immense et les yeux de la bête paraissent sortir d'un autre monde ... bouche cruelle mais quelque chose de fort et de beau. *Yeux sortant de la nuit"* (Striking. Beauty and the beast. An enormous mane and the beast's eyes seem to be emerging from another world ..., a cruel mouth but something strong and beautiful. *Eyes coming out of the night*). Repeatedly this nighttime figure occurred among our subjects, not only on Card IV, but also on Cards I, V, and VI as well, mostly characterized as a monster or a bird of prey and death, but sometimes in other terms, once as the *croque-mitaine* himself, another time as a German or Russian with heavy boots (Card IV). The war-orphaned French children also saw ogres, serpents, and big men on the achromatic Rorschach blots. They also tended to make direct reference to the blackness of blots more than did either the English or Spanish refugee children.

The Desire to Overcome Fear of Strangeness and Darkness by Seeing with Special Clarity

The French prohibition against the child's nocturnal curiosity seems to have the effect of stimulating an intense wish to see everything clearly and distinctly. Our informants commented repeatedly on the relative vagueness or clearness of their perceptual images of the blots, such as "imprécis" (not precise), "très vague" (very vague), "impressionnant" (striking), "plus net" (clearer), "nettement" (clearly), "sans aucune possibilité d'erreur" (without any possibility of error), "précis" (precise), "voilà quelque chose de définitif" (now there is something definite), "raisonnable" (reasonable), etc. Sometimes a blot which was interpreted as something menacing and vague was later perceived with satisfaction as something clear, precise, and less of a threat. One subject who saw Card IV as roughly and vaguely representing the *croque-mitaine*, later noticed the small replica of the blot on the Rorschach location chart and said: "Tout à fait un gorille" (absolutely a gorilla). Another informant who perceived in Card IV an ominous bird of prey and death, also caught a glimpse of the replica of the blot on the location chart (seen through the sheet which was by chance held up toward the light by the examiner). His comment was, "Voilà le monstre très net qui part dans sa caverne" (There is the monster very clear, going off to his cave). In both cases the perceptual image was made clearer by the reduced size (and hence safeness) of the blot. In the second instance, the creature was made less terrifying by appearing to fly away, whereas in the original response the creature was described as attacking. Also, on the location chart the blots are less black than they are on the plates and give less an effect of shading.

Responses to the Thematic Apperception Test also illustrate the re-evocation of childhood nocturnal curiosity and the desire to try to see clearly and distinctly in a threatening situation. One subject introduces the longed-for light into a dark picture of a man and woman embracing (TAT Card 10), "L'homme embrasse la femme … c'est le soir, il y a la lumière" (The man embraces the woman … it is evening, there is a light). Elsewhere another subject sees a mother looking with "un regard inquisiteur" (with an inquisitive look) into her child's bed-room (TAT Card 5). There is something "bizarre" about it; there is light where there should be darkness and vice versa (one may guess that the subject is disturbed also by another reversal: in the background recall which is evoked, it was the child rather than the mother who was doing the nighttime looking).

This emphasis on trying to see clearly and distinctly as a result of parental repressing of the child's nocturnal curiosity may be reflected in more sublimated form in the intellectual emphasis on clear and distinct ideas and lucidity of expression both in formal education and in child rearing in the home. This emphasis on lucidity is also seen in French philosophy, notably Descartes.

One characteristic of the paintings of French children (ages 13-16) and in the free drawing on the Horn-Hellersberg test (drawing No. 13) is the tipping up of horizontal planes, reducing a three-dimensional vista to a flat two-dimensional design (a characteristic of French painting, particularly still life since near the beginning of the century). There are no distant horizons or unbounded areas and expanses of sea, sky and fields in these paintings and drawings as we commonly find among drawings of many American adolescents. In other words, there is relative absence of linear perspective, of objects diminishing in size with distance, or of atmospheric effects. The most remote objects are in this way brought close and seen clearly and distinctly. Thus, we see through a different medium than that of inkblots an attempt to handle the problem we have been discussing of reducing vagueness and increasing clarity of perception and hence clearness of understanding.

Distantiation

Another repeated mode of response on the part of all of our French subjects to the Rorschach plates was the tendency to distantiate animal, and more especially human, figures when they occurred. This distantiation took place in space and time and with marked preference for remoteness as exemplified by mythological figures. It was striking how rarely the adults and also the war orphan children saw human figures in the cards. Instead, they favored giants, monsters, goblins (*lutins*), gnomes, chimeras, and other mythological creations. One subject sees in Card IX, "des lutins ... ils ont une origine mythologique, des farfadelles fictives" (goblins ... they have a mythological origin, imaginary elves). This subject also perceives in Card X, "des sorciers avec une barbe. Ils me font penser au Cardinal Richelieu" (sorcerers with a beard. They make me think of Cardinal Richelieu). Another sees in Card I, "des espèces de génies avec leurs deux yeux" (sorts of genies with their two eyes)· Another sees in Card II, "deux magistrats, médecins russes, comédie de Molière ... toge noir d'avocat" (two magistrates, Russian physicians, comedy of Molière ... black toga of the lawyer). Remoteness in time is emphasized by the subject who interprets Card I (upside down) as, "le bourgeois sous Louis Philippe, il y a cent ans ... être grotesque" (the bourgeois under Louis Philippe, a hundred years ago ... grotesque being), or by the informant who sees in Card VII, "une forme préhistorique, animale ... les archéologistes les trouvaient ... on les trouve dans les ruines" (a prehistoric form, animal ... archeologists find them ... they are found in ruins). For distantiation in space we find a response to Card V, of "chauve-souris d'un pays tropical" (bat of a tropical country), and another to Card I, "coléoptère des environs d'une source du Nil... on ne les a presque jamais vus" (coleopter from around the sources of the Nile ... they have almost never been seen)· Other subjects perceive exotic humans, Negroes with a curl and fish offering, Bantus, Eskimos, and Arabs. The war-orphaned children described figures (Card III) as "bonshommes avec pantoufles" (little men with slippers); (Card IV) "Babar quand il pleure" (Babar when he cries); (Card V) "rochers avec des hommes-phares" (rocks with men-lighthouses); (Card IX) "magiciens avec des grands manteaux" (magicians with big coats).

Another way we found in which French subjects dehumanized human figures was to characterize them as toys (made of wood, velvet, plush), puppets, ornaments, or to describe them as stylized, "drôle" (comic), "excentrique" (eccentric), "comique" (comic). On the few thematic apperception stories we obtained, there is also this tendency to distantiate, to label characters as unreal, as dream figures or those in a film plot or fairy tale.

Careful reading of interview material uncovers occasional instances of the distantiating defense. For instance, a middle-aged male informant, after blocking severely on the question of the father's role in the French family, and attempting to deny the father's importance, shifts his ground to speak of the French countryside, which he compares to the "old villa *romaine.*" After introducing these effects of distance in space and time, and the additional distantiating device of his higher learning, he is able to speak of parental authority, and says that on these farms the authority of the father is "absolutely complete." However, the interview situation does not so often evoke the emotional disturbances for which this defense is employed; and one would not have noticed it in the interviews if one had not become aware of it from its much more frequent occurrence on the Rorschach.

Immobilization of Human Movement

Another consistent feature of our French Rorschach records is the scarcity of animal and human movement, rather particularly the latter. It would seem that as soon as these subjects see the possibility of some activity or aggression, they freeze the figure, pin it down, or transform it to stone. Thus, one individual perceives a savage animal (Card VIII), but the only action that he attributes to it is that of looking at something. Even this is too dangerous and he reconstructs the perceptual image as a tiger seen on the edge of a precipice and it stops. The dangers of looking may perhaps be referred here again to the child's nocturnal curiosity. Another subject sees a monster, but then immediately transforms it into a mountain, a rock worn by time. This becomes still further frozen and etherealized into strange designs in ice. The same subject sees a bat in flight, then quickly shifts to seeing it pinned down (Card V); when she sees two animals she transforms them into handles of a vase (Card VIII). Another informant sees in Card III two figures, a child's toy, that do not move of their own volition. Another subject starts to see movement in an inanimate object, an "espèce de girouette" (a sort of top), but he says it is only partly moving, partly standing still, and then he transforms his perceptual image and sees the same blot area as the "croix de Lorraine" (cross of Lorraine). A war orphan speaks of (Card II) "deux personnes attachées par une main, assises" (two people attached by one hand, sitting), or again (Card III) "deux messieurs regardent un homme mort" (two men looking at a dead man). Another child (Card IV) perceives "un animal écrasé" (a crushed animal); another (Card V), "un papillon épinglé" (a butterfly pinned down).

The presumably strong French cathexis of painting and perhaps the specific interest in *nature morte* (still life) may also be an expression of defense against aggressive tendencies; picturing the result of the aggressive act (the immobilized object) rather than the act itself. Also, in figure painting, one gets the immobilized human figure. If any violent action is shown, it is displaced to an exotic locale (distantiation, e.g., Delacroix).

Another manner in which our French informants expressed conflict about aggressive impulses was not to freeze or immobilize animal and human movement but to give alternative answers, one the more directly expressive of possible hostility-fear feelings than the other. The subject appears to manifest inability to decide between two evoked perceptual images. We have already given an instance of a bat in flight or "épinglé" (pinned down, made less dangerous). Another informant sees (Card II) two black dogs who "trempent leurs pattes dans le sirop de framboise *ou* dans le *sang*" (dip their paws in strawberry syrup *or* in *blood*); and she reports, concerning the outer red blots in Card III, "deux chats qui sont en train de tomber *ou* on les a jetés par la fenêtre, les pauvres chats" (two cats which are in the act of falling *or* they have been thrown from the window, the poor cats). Again, another individual sees in the red on Card II, "quelque chose d'un peu choquant, tache de sang *ou* je passe tout de suite au terrain géographique" (something a little shocking, a stain of blood or I move on right away to geographic terrain). Another subject sees on Card IV, "têtes de deux femmes, amusantes expressions *ou* qui se fâchant" (heads of two women, amusing expressions *or* who are angry).

In the paintings by the French children we see the tendency to present people, if at all, with very little human action. The most active figures are an incidental diver and swimmer in a river scene. In the one sports picture, tennis players are standing still waiting for the game to begin.

The most rapidly moving human figures are people being swung by a revolving swing at a fair; they are not moving on their own initiative but are being moved by an outside agency. In one of the Horn-Hellersberg drawings a mountain and an arrow are depicted. The child states that a man (not shown) has shot an arrow at a bird (not shown) but he misses. Thus, no figure is shown either doing the shooting or toward whom the missile is directed. This absence of forceful human movement in other materials reinforces the results of our Rorschach protocols.

These tendencies we have been discussing – dehumanization of figures, distantiation, and immobilizing and toning down animal and especially human movement – may possibly be interpreted as a repression of aggression. One's own aggression is dangerous and must be brought under control. That the French are afraid of breaking out into open hostility (in action, not in words), are taught control and repression of expressions of anger ("pas de drames" – no scenes), and are prevented from fighting it out or defending themselves in childhood quarrels, has been brought out time and again in our interview material. Physical fights among girls are inadmissible. They may start among boys but they are not to be tolerated. "Disputez-vous mais ne vous battez pas" (Quarrel but do not fight) is a reminder that is given by adults to children. Adults are expected to step in and stop fighting on the part of children; these adults may be members of the family, teachers, or strangers who pass in the street and witness a fight.

One of the hypotheses developed early in our study and substantiated further in subsequent interviews is that the object of education in France is to maximize *bonheur* (perhaps *bien être* is a preferable term), and minimize *malheur* in adult life and this cannot be achieved without skills (learning). But skills are not adequate alone; they must be supplemented by control; for it is only by continuous control that the precarious and dignified status of full humanity can be maintained. The main spheres where control should be exercised are the body (*tenue* – deportment; *savoir-faire* – skillful management) and the emotions. Emotions should not be excessive, nor should one abandon oneself to their sway. One of the major techniques for controlling the emotions is verbalization, as in "disputez-vous mais ne vous battez pas." Thus, it would appear that some of the ways the French may control their possibly aroused feelings and emotions when perceiving the Rorschach blots is by making the kinds of responses we have been describing, responses that suggest the warding off of danger; that render things remote, vague, at a distance in time and space; and that immobilize creatures, animals, and people who might threaten them and/or to whom they feel hostilely inclined.

Repression of and Outlets for Oral and Motor Aggression

Recurring content in the Rorschach protocols was shellfish – crabs or lobsters (the word *homard* was used, not *langouste*) – frequently with *pinces* (claws) specifically mentioned. Sometimes only the *pinces* were seen. The subjects seemed to have some feeling about these crabs and lobsters which they did not express verbally, but rather by laughter as they gave their responses. One may hypothecate that one sees here a clue to the French solution to oral aggression, that we have an indirect outlet for aggression which has become fixated or has regressed to the oral level, aggression which the formidable control the French use over their impulses does not entirely succeed in repressing. Thus, oral aggressive tendencies are (as is usual) projected onto a retaliating animal (the biting crab or lobster), but this animal in turn becomes something good to eat. These biting shellfish may be supposed to have an additional emotional significance for the French for this reason. Characteristically, our subjects did not see the shellfish as either biting or being bitten. In their elliptical way they focused their feelings onto the perceptual image of the object, suppressing or repressing the action associated with it. These shellfish are generally described passively as just *being there* but possessing *pinces* (craws). One subject emphasizes the *pinces* by calling the red blots of Card II "des pinces supplémentaires" (supplementary claws), having seen a regular set of claws in the black center.

Further evidence for the diffusion of such responses is that these marine animals or their appendages were projected onto any one of the ten Rorschach plates. Among the French war orphans there were also instances of seeing heads and *"pinces"* (claws) of *"homard"* (lobster) and *"écrevisse"* (crayfish). In addition, one little girl (age 12-1/2) saw (Card II) a "rhinocéros avec la défense qu'ils ont" (rhinoceros with the defense they have); and another girl (age 13) saw "un homme qui tire la langue" (a man who sticks out his tongue), each case suggesting oral aggressive tendencies. One of our adult subjects, however, came out more boldly and described the attacking quality of the claws; he imagined the whole blot in Card I to be "un masque grimaçant et grotesque, terminé par des pinces de crabes qui lui rongent le cerveau" (a mask grimacing and grotesque, terminated by the claws of crabs which are gnawing his brain). This same subject gives as his response to Card IV "monstre de caverne, une tête et yeux d'homard" (cave monster, head and eyes of a lobster).

In relation to oral aggression, one may recall another successful sublimated employment of it by the French in their high cultivation of verbal aggression – biting wit.

Color Responses

In spite of what appears to be inhibition and repression of aggressive impulses as suggested by the quality and content of many of the Rorschach responses of our French informants, most of them responded freely to the color on the inkblots. Eight of our ten adult informants gave a marked preponderance of color answers in the standard movement-color ratio; one gave more movement than color, and one was ambi-equal but very productive of both human movement and color. This tendency to be responsive to and make use of color suggests, according to Rorschach theory, that our subjects were able to form warm relationships with people (at least in the immediate world around them, such as in their *foyers)* and to obtain pleasure from external stimulation (i. e., food, clothes, art, sex objects). They appear less afraid of stimulation from the outer world than from their fantasies brought about from inner promptings (assuming human movement responses to the blots indicative of promptings from within, as attested to by Rorschach theory). Nor do the French subjects go to pieces in their response to color. They exert control by giving form-color answers (i. e., birds of paradise with beautiful plumage, ornamental vases, costumed characters in plays, flowers that grow in the woods in the spring) interspersed with some freer, less controlled color-form responses (in which color rather than form determines the response), shown in such perceptual images as "pink cotton candy," "color of autumn leaves," "salad." Even when giving more intense and disorganized pure color responses (no clearness of form), such as "blood" or "putrid meat," these French informants come back into balance and control by following their disorganized and diffuse response by a well-organized one in which color is still used, not repressed, but brought into line and control. One subject sees in Card II, something "facilement obscène, adaptation du sexe avec le sang" (easily obscene, adaptation of sex with blood). He then modifies his response to perceiving "deux magistrats, médecins russes, comédie de Molière" (two magistrates, Russian physicians, comedy of Molière). Another sees an open wound and broken bone (Card II) and then follows this response by describing "une espèce de gâteau à la crème" (a sort of cake with cream).

Just as they control their aggressive feelings by distantiation and immobilization of movement, so do the French subjects control their responses to color by making the form of their responses precise and clear. But it is through color (and hence, according to Rorschach theory, from the outer world) that they show the most freedom and have the most outlet for enjoyment. (In Rorschach terms it is suggested that their *Erlebnistypus* is more extraversive than introversive.) This recalls the way in which Proust's remembrances had to be set going by the taste of the *madeleine* dipped in tea, or by the sudden glimpse of a church spire.

Our French orphans were not, as were our adults, preponderantly extraversive in their modes of responding to the inkblots. Tulchin and Levy found that the English war refugee children they tested were predominantly introversive (ratio M:C was 1.5 : 1.0), while the Spanish refugee children were more extraversive (ratio M:C was .07 : 1.3). Using the same ratio, we found the French war orphans to be ambiequal (ratio M:C was 1.4 : 1.5). Since all three groups of children gave very few human movement or color responses the differences between them are only suggestive and have little statistical reliability. Also, we do not feel we can compare the results of our adults with those of the children. The adults not only were more intelligent, but were more open and freer both in number and quality of their responses. We must not forget that the children were refugees, living away from home, who had had severe traumatic experiences. They could not be expected to respond as freely to the test situation as would children living in their homes and in a more stable environment.

Conclusion

As we stated earlier, we are not forming conclusions about the results of our projective material from French subjects. We have offered suggestions and made hypotheses about personality-in-culture from the data we did obtain and to which we had access. We trust that others as well as ourselves may be stimulated to substantiate or disprove the points we have raised, to take issue with or complement our ideas and to bring in other ideas and hypotheses.

NOTES

1. For a review of some of the problems involved in the use of projective tests in cultural analyses, cf. Theodora M. Abel, "The Rorschach Test in the Study of Cultures," *Rorschach Research Exchange and Journal of Projective Techniques,* vol. 12, No. 2, 1948, pp. 79-93.
2. Cf. Theodora M. Abel and Francis L. K. Hsu, "Some Aspects of Personality of Chinese as Revealed by the Rorschach Test," *Rorschach Research Exchange and Journal of Projective Techniques,* vol. 13, No. 3, 1949, pp. 28~01.
3. Our French data, which concern us here, are meager. We have detailed Rorschach protocols (in French) on ten of our informants, and five Thematic Apperception protocols. In addition, we have had access to twelve Rorschach protocols, accompanied by Binet protocols of French war orphans in an orphanage in Switzerland. These children were also given the Horn-Hellersberg drawing test. (The material on the French orphans was made available to us by Mrs. Ruth Métraux.) The Horn-Hellersberg drawings were all treated as free drawings rather than in terms of scoring categories worked out for the test, and were taken into consideration in the present investigation as a sample of nonverbal projective material to be compared especially with the paintings by French children exhibited at the Museum of Modern Art in New York during the winter of 1947-48. For some crosscultural comparisons we used the study of Rorschachs by S. H. Tulchin and D. M. Levy ("Rorschach Test Differences in a Group of

Spanish and English Refugee Children," *American Journal of Orthopsychiatry,* vol. 15, No. 2, 1945, pp. 361-68).

Our adult sample included very little homogeneous material beyond the fact that our ten informants were French. There were six women and four men; all of them were born in or near Paris, but one was educated in Central France, another in North Africa. Yet another had moved to army posts during his childhood from one end of France and her colonies to the other. Seven informants were Catholic, two were part Jewish, one was Protestant. The socioeconomic level of the ten informants varied from small bourgeoisie to aristocracy. Two of the informants were facial plastic war casualties in America for surgery. Two were war brides, one happily married to an American, the other on her way home to Casablanca, having left her American husband. The common factor of our adult informants was that of living, temporarily at least, in New York City and their willingness to act as informants and take a projective test.

The suggestions we obtained and which will be discussed were formulated mainly as a result of the Rorschach protocols of the adult informants, confirmatory material coming, from the Thematic Apperception protocols of these adults, the Rorschach responses and drawings of the French war orphans, and the paintings of French children.

With our small and varied samples of children and adults, any quantitative generalizations in terms of Rorschach scoring categories would, of course, be out of the question. Consequently, we wish to emphasize that the material is largely qualitative, that it does not have statistical reliability, that it is suggestive and hypothetical. At the same time, it should be added that we found the Rorschach and Thematic Apperception protocols, as well as the children's drawings, stimulating and fruitful during our discussions, which centered mainly around interview material from our informants, and congruent with our findings in analyses of other types of material, i.e., films, novels, etc.

BIBLIOGRAPHY

Abel, Theodora M. "The Rorschach Test in the Study of Cultures," *Rorschach Research Exchange and Journal of Projective Techniques,* vol. 12, No. 2, 1948, pp. 79-93.

Abel, Theodora M. and Francis L. K. Hsu. "Some Aspects of Personality of Chinese as Revealed by the Rorschach Test," *Rorschach Exchange and Journal of Projective Techniques,* vol. 13, No. 3, 1949, pp. 285-301.

Tulchin, S. H. and D. M. Levy. "Rorschach Test Differences in a Group of Spanish and English Refugee Children," *American Journal of Orthopsychiatry,* vol. 15, No. 2, 1945, pp. 361-388.